Silence on the Bridge

Silence on the Bridge

Leda Stegel

VANTAGE PRESS
New York

Cover design by Susan Thomas

FIRST EDITION

All rights reserved, including the right of
reproduction in whole or in part in any form.

Copyright © 2005 by Leda Stegel

Published by Vantage Press, Inc.
419 Park Ave. South, New York, NY 10016

Manufactured in the United States of America
ISBN: 0-533-14928-2

Library of Congress Catalog Card No.: 2004092868

0 9 8 7 6 5 4 3 2 1

To my mother, a brave woman, whose sole purpose was the welfare of her family. She knew deep inside she was not going to escape the tragedies and sorrows that fate had in store for her. She saw the future, she tried to change it for the best, only to eventually lose everything precious to her. She could foresee the future, but she felt her own predictions were working against her and felt she could not help *la forza del destino,* the forces of destiny, just like in the opera. She felt our life was already written and even with trying we could not change dramatically the course of our life.

To my father, the optimist, who remained hopeful throughout life and our family losses. Even in the worst of times he could always say: "What can be done?" then proceed with the task, and he always found a way. He believed in a happier future and the conviction that we make our life. He told me many times: "Don't be upset, just laugh, life is too short." His saying was: *"La vita comincia domani,"* life begins tomorrow. My mother's was: *"La vita é un sogno sfuggente,"* life is a fleeting dream. They wrote these sayings in my memory book before I left for the USA.

This is a gift to my children and their children to help them understand their heritage.

Contents

Foreword   ix
Preface   xi
Introduction Bridges   xv

1. The War   1
2. The Picture   3
3. Homes in Fiume   5
4. The Simple Life   12
5. Neighborhood   17
6. Special Holidays   21
7. World War I   24
8. Ornella   27
9. Happy Childhood Then a Fading Dream   31
10. Sergio, My Brother   35
11. The Boots   37
12. The Letter   41
13. The Loss   44
14. The Good Life   46
15. The Bombing   49
16. My Father's Youth   51
17. Zio Pepi, Uncle   56
18. New Home   59
19. Gypsy Oracle   62
20. The Stories of the Operas   65
21. My Mother   69
22. The Hungarians   73
23. Soltesz Family   76
24. Paolo Soltesz, My Grandfather   81
25. A Portrait   84

26.	Paolo Soltesz (My Uncle)	87
27.	My Brother, Ireneo/Pippi	89
28.	Silent Movie	92
29.	**Borsa Nera** (Black Market)	95
30.	A Life of Perils	113
31.	The Psychic	115
32.	The Jews	118
33.	Silence at Susak Bridge	121
34.	Partisans	125
35.	Ireneo	127
36.	The Funeral	129
37.	Camps	130
38.	The Revenge of the Partisans	132
39.	**Arrivederci** Fiume	134
40.	Life in an Institution	137
41.	My Life in Firenze	140
42.	Via Silvio Pellico	142
43.	The Vacation	148
44.	Zia Irene	151
45.	**Villa Vittoria**	155
46.	Agape	165
47.	Food for Thought	168
48.	The Decision	171
49.	Un Sogno (A Dream)	174
50.	Good-bye **Italia, Arrivederci!**	178
51.	The Center	183
52.	Suddenly, No Family	190
53.	The Arrival	193
54.	New Beginnings	195
55.	**La Forza del Destino** (The Force of Destiny)	201
56.	Representative Pelley	204
57.	Alone	207

Foreword

Dear Leda,

    I must congratulate you on your determination to set down the incredible story of your family. It is a story—a wealth of stories—well worth the telling; quite unlike anything I have previously read. And I read a great deal!

    You have the ability to do this work with dignity and grace—you have a sensitivity that is uniquely your own, a rather melancholic nostalgic for a place, for the people and the times in which they lived. That is the essence of a true memoir.

    I hope with all my greedy little heart that someday I may be fortunate enough to see this work completed.

Marjorie Rommel
An English Teacher

Sept. 30-00

Preface

One of my ambitions is to write a book. This thought started many years ago when I was taking courses in English for my nursing degree. Growing up "here and there," I really never had a continuous education that was not interrupted by some event. Now, I was getting my real education. The first goal was to be able to have a profession. I worked as a waitress to pay for my college education and finally became an R.N. in 1975. My profession is not only rewarding, but gave me independence.

My second goal is to write about my experiences clearly, in a way hopefully easy and interesting to read, and also informatively. It is amazing how far back one can remember, at least in my case. I can see scenes and episodes from when I was three, four or five years old. I want to write a book that speaks about my family as far back as I remember.

It would almost appear I came from nowhere. I can account only for my sister, Wilma, who lives near me in Tacoma. I had no uncles, aunts, cousins or other relatives living in America. In Europe, there are only four cousins and their descendants.

Life is not always happy. For this reason, I could not start writing. I was afraid to be sad again. This held me back for several years. This all changed when I was in a creative writing class. I found out I could write episodes that were fun to read and were meaningful. I overcame my fear of writing about the past. Gibran said in his book: "Where there is sadness, look deeper, and there is joy." The sadness was not there anymore, and I did not find myself crying all the time. Instead, I found joy in remembering all the significant people in my life.

When I was young, I loved to read adventure books about the American Indians and their wars and I loved the *Three Musketeers*. Now, my favorite books are from John Grisham, Paul Theroux, and best of all *Into Thin Air* by John Krakauer.

I came to the United States in 1951 when I was fifteen years old. I came here with my sister, two years younger, as refugee children of postwar Europe. The war devastated our family. In a supremely unselfish act, our parents decided to let us emigrate, hoping for a better life for us. In their distress, they could only envision a life with little hope for an education or a job-training if we stayed in Italy. For a short time just before coming to U.S., I worked in the office of the company where my father was employed. No doubt people were trying to help us while my father was unable to work. At age fifteen, I lacked the skills that were needed to earn a paycheck.

Neither of our parents were in good health, either physically or mentally. They were distressed by the loss of two sons and by a life that was becoming more difficult with the loss of earnings due to my father's illness (he contracted tuberculosis). He had spent the war years in a concentration camp (a forced-labor camp) in Germany.

After much processing and paperwork, my sister and I came to live in Bremerton with two older sisters who were both high school teachers. One was a widow and the other never married. June and Winifred came to live together in life when June lost her husband.

Whenever I say one word, people ask me where I am

from. This after forty years in this country! I am from Italy originally, but this area now. It is of little consequence where one is from, rather, what makes a person is experiences and how one responds to them, people that have touched our life, events, places. Where we are from originally may fade away as unimportant. Accents are just an interesting type of speech pattern that should not interfere at all with what a person is saying.

Life is a fleeting dream. This is why I feel I have to catch this dream before it ends and memory fades. I have to leave a written account of my family.

It seems long ago that my mother was trying to tell me of her youth and her life. I was too young. Then she was gone before I was able to understand. My mind was always on matters like what to wear next day to school, assignment not finished, anxiety over catching the little train to school early in the morning. Somehow, I must have heard because now I remember and I can see how remarkable my mother and father were.

My life is different enough to want to write about it. I feel I need to have some kind of written history for my descendants and for myself. I have lost so much that now I have to write so as to never forget.

Right now, I see my mother and I walking in the city. I remember her saying, "You see that sign? You will soon see how wonderful it is to be able to read it." I was four years old.

On one of my latest trips to Italy I visited the city where I was born. Most of all, I wanted to see where my brother was killed, the little village of Buie, not far from Fiume (Rijeka).

It brought back memories of my mother and I traveling in that area to the farms, bartering for food. In those hills, there were a lot of partisans and Germans fighting during the war.

On this trip, I found the *Divina Commedia* by Dante Alighieri, a book I studied in school paragraph per paragraph, as it is a complicated and clever allegory. However, I did not find *La Biblioteca dei Ragazzi* by Emilio Salgari. It was a series of books for the upper grade school children.

Life goes on, there is joy and sadness and also the future. I have so much to be thankful for—my sons, always good babies, toddlers, teenagers and adults, and their father who always believed in me. My greatest wish is for all our four boys, my sister's and ours, to be good friends and share each other's life experiences. To help each other as they did in their paper routes, in snow and sickness, and be there for each other always.

Introduction
Bridges

Something is very intriguing, even spiritual, about bridges. People admire bridges and are proud if they are lucky enough to be building bridges. Almost every day, there is a report on the new Narrow bridge in Tacoma. Being part in building a bridge is an experience not forgotten.

A bridge is the first target for the military. It is a connection between two important places. Sometimes it is the place chosen for leaving this world and enter into another. It is a special meeting place sometimes.

In this book, it is a place that brings both good and bad tidings and I will never forget this bridge. Hence the title of this manuscript . . . *Silence on the Bridge.*

It was an old stone bridge, probably built by the Romans. It divided two cities: Fiume and Susak. The little river was really just a creek coming from the mountains, draining to the Gulf of the Quarnero with the port able to hold 150 large ships. The stone bridge was low with barely an incline from the "piazza" on the Fiume side, or also called the Tersatto sector of the city. The stone arch under the bridge was typical of many in Italy. Florence has many large bridges of this style, one of which has little shops built right on the bridge.

The Dalmatian coast was one of the summer residences for the Romans. Diocleziano (Diocletian) was the emperor who built an entire city in Split. No doubt the Romans went through Fiume.

My mother holding me with her arm around me in silence, we waited till it was very dark and quiet, and we were all alone.

Silence on the Bridge

1
The War

When the war broke out, I was four years old. I remember when I heard the cries of the older children, "The war started, the war started." They were going up and down the streets screaming as if to let everyone know. Of course, it was all over the radio stations, but the children were excited and thought they were providing a valuable public service. I don't know what was going on in their heads, but I wasn't too thrilled. I had seen serious men in our house too many times, with their ears on the radios. Their discussions appeared to me anxious and worried.

My father and his fellow coworkers or friends often gathered at our house to discuss politics. Our house was a busy place in the evenings, sometimes, and noisy too. At times, I would go in my parents' bedroom and look at the picture at the head of their bed a long time, and I would feel at peace. That picture had been there ever since I remembered. The Madonna is kneeling beside her child in his bed and the baby is peacefully sleeping.

I studied the features of the mother of Jesus. She has an anxious look and tears in her eyes. This picture which I stared at for a long time gave me a sense of comfort at the same time some anxiety. But why was she crying? Did she know already of the fate of her son? I still loved that picture so very much. It was a comfort to me on the long evening of political discussion in the kitchen when I could not sleep.

This was when the war years started. When the air raids began, the sirens became a familiar sound. It never failed to bring a deep fear inside me. Most of the time, I could hear the airplane bombers approaching long before the wail of the sirens would begin. It always brought anxiety and my legs would become weak when I heard the muffled roar of the airplanes in the distance. I remember my mother was always surprised when I told her the airplane were coming because she could not hear them. Nobody else could hear them as I did.

Some days, the sirens would be going off very often, like four or five times a day. Each time, we would all run to the underground shelter that served our neighborhood. My brother Ireneo would carry my sister Wilma on his shoulder and pull me by the hand. Sometimes, he even tried to carry me too on his arms while Wilma was on his neck. Mother would limp behind us and father was at the foundry in their own shelters.

There were many such shelters throughout the city, each typically an underground cave since the natural terrain of the whole area is solid rock filled with natural tunnels and caverns. The caverns were prepared like the rounded mines of the ore prospectors in the hills of Idaho as I have seen them from the rafts trips. This region around Fiume (Rijeka) is called Carso. Not far from there are the famous Grotte di Postumia in Slovenia. Looking at a map today, I have difficulty finding these villages or cities because all the familiar names have been changed and are now Yugoslavia and more recently, Croatia. For example, a nearby vacation city, Abbazia, is now Opatija. The little town of Buie is now Buje, Pola is Pula, and Postumia is now Postojna. My world was only Fiume.

2
The Picture

The second picture in the photo section is of my family when I was very small. I am certain my aunt, Irene, the only one in the family who owned a camera, took it. She loved taking photos. It is because of her that we have some pictures of our past. Aunt Irene had to travel most of a day on a train to visit us as she lived and worked in Milano and we lived in Fiume, on the other side of northern Italy.

In the photo, my father and my mother stand proudly with my two older brothers, Ireneo and Sergio. One brother is fourteen years old and the other ten. My sister Wilma is in my mother's arms and is about one year old. My father is holding me and I am about three.

It is the most wonderful and warm picture. I can see the love of my dear aunt who posed us all and then returned to her spot to snap the picture. She would cherish this photo until her next visit, as she was alone and had no family of her own.

This may have been the last happy picture of our family. It was taken before the war, when our family was still together with no idea of what was to come. My father, standing tall beside my mother, posed in front of our house before it was bombed out.

The camera my aunt used was one of the old-fashioned Kodak with the accordion bellows. She would hold it at waist level and look down into the viewer. The old camera showed everything upside down as in a way everything soon would be when our world as we knew it then would vanish.

I remember well the heavy, warm beige coat and scarf I was wearing, taken off in this picture to show my sailor blouse. Many of our clothes came from Milano or were home made by my mother. My sister wore a homemade knit coat, blue and red, with no buttons, only two strings to draw it together. My father was in his best jacket and my mother in her best clothes. My brothers wore the regular boys attire of that era, good solid clothes of heavy wool fabric.

The picture is in black and white, but the colors in my mind are vivid.

3

Homes in Fiume

My early childhood is the most wonderful part of my memory. Childhood is an important phase of our life. It is amazing to me that I would remember age four or five or even younger so well. I realize only now how much a child can assimilate and retain for the rest of his life. I noticed that children that had a good wholesome childhood become very happy adults. Children need to grow up in a nurturing home, they deserve it. The first few years belong to the child, to enjoy and learn about their world. My mother said, "They didn't ask to come into the world." She'd say this of neglected children. Now that they have them, their parents are responsible for them, was her strong attitude. She was very worried of children being neglected. I heard her say, "This girl is well brought up." (*Questa bambina é ben portata su") of the children she approved.*

I don't remember being scolded or disciplined. I only remember wonderful times of playing with dolls or other toys that my brother made for us. We were taught manners and respect early and there wasn't anything to be scolded for. We knew what was expected. Our life was much simpler than it is for children today. Our toys and activities consisted of setting up store on shelves we made ourselves. We'd gather weeds and grains or seeds, berries, and small rocks. Some size of rocks represented potatoes. Then other children would come and buy these goods with paper money.

There were other homemade or invented games, like

playing theater. We acted little plays on a madeup stage, dressing up with mother's clothes, father's tools and anything we could find. We always would take turns in being actors or spectators.

The setting of my town is similar to Tacoma, Washington. Fiume, or Rijeka, is much older than Tacoma. This ancient city located on the border of Yugoslavia and Italy then is now part of Croatia. The city has an important working port, just like Tacoma. During WWI, Fiume was under Austro-Hungarian rule, then later Italian, and now Croatian. I was born here when it was part of Italy in 1935, and all the inhabitants spoke Italian. However, because it was a border city, most of these people also spoke Slovenian, Croatian, and German, as well as other languages. There were many Hungarians here also. Of course, children went to Italian schools, and no other language was offered.

My mother was Hungarian and my father's family was Slovenian. My father was born in Fiume, so he was legally Italian. My mother never considered herself to be Italian, but only Hungarian. She was eighteen years old when she came to Fiume from Budapest and she never spoke Italian perfectly. In some sentences many words were out of sequence, but her pronunciation was almost perfect.

Fiume was built by the Romans. In antiquity, the city was erected on the hill named *Tersatto* and, in fact, it was originally called *Tersatica*. It was built in defense of the valley between the mountains and the sea. From 1860 to 1918, Fiume was under the control of the Austro-Hungarian empire, but had an autonomous government. Fiume was never part of the Slavic group of countries—Croatia, Slovenia, Serbia, and other small Slavic countries. Because the city had always been autonomous, it remained under its modern name of Fiume, the Italian word for river. Unfortunately, since WWII the city is called Rijeka, and is part of Croatia.

Fiume's center core, called *Citta Vecchia* (old town), was the original city where many people lived and were mostly poor and had lived there for generations. They had dwellings that were passed down to the next line in the family.

Citta Vecchia was an interesting place when I was small but not a place where we would go often, and never without our parents. It was easy to lose track of children running in the small little streets, and mothers then as today were fearful of their children being stolen. Mother had a strong hold of our hands if we went there.

Buildings were only two, three, or four stories high, with cobblestone streets, very narrow and hilly. It was like a maze and a child could be easily lost. Laundry crossed over the streets, hung high on ropes and pulleys. The streets were lined with little places to eat and shops selling bread, meat and vegetables. Each little store specialized in one item, such as meat of a different cut or a store with varieties of breads. There was also an open air market where the farmers brought in their goods.

Apartments and living quarters were located above the shops, and people went into the streets to buy and barter every day for fresh goods. It was very noisy on every little street one went to, either with music and crowds of people talking loudly. There were little arguments in every corner, it seemed to me, with shouting very often. Crescendo of voices here and there, and open loud discussions. *Citta Vecchia* was not for children, and I went there only a few times with my mother.

To get to downtown Fiume we had to take a long ride on a street car on a rail. The center of the city was several miles from where we lived. The rail for the train was below the hillside, running along the waterfront and the shipyard. The port area was in the city proper and it was a busy port. From the hill above the city we could see big stacks, ships at the docks and continuous traffic in the bay with big and small boats.

This very busy area, not far from *Citta Vecchia,* was the heart of the city. It was crowded with the people of Fiume, foreign sailors, as well as Italians.

Near the port square was an impressive church of gothic architecture, faced with red stucco and bilateral tiered staircase to the entrance. It is still a landmark featured in postcards.

Fiume was surrounded by hillsides sprawling with houses and apartments where working middle-class lived.

We lived in a corner apartment on the bottom floor, part of two-story building containing ten units. We had a neighbor above us and another alongside, followed by a row of others. This arrangement would be called a condominium today, or in Italian, a *caseggiato*. We never heard the family upstairs from us and we didn't know them very well. Next door to us lived a professor, his wife, and a daughter whom we rarely saw.

This home was in *Via* F. Redi. Francesco Redi was a writer. This home was the warmest part of my childhood. Our family was all together and some relatives were close by, so we could visit.

No one had a house all to themselves, as is common in the USA. It was always the dream of our parents to have their own house. I remember going with them to the very outskirts of Fiume, very far from where we lived, to look at a small lot in the middle of nowhere. There was talk of building a house on this lot, they talked quietly about it while I was standing nearby. Of course, it never happened, but often, we still went to look at the place. We could have used a lot of space around us. Our family was big with four children, in comparison to the rest of our aunts and uncles. There were only a very few families with many children, usually fascists trying to please *Il Duce*. Most of our aunts and uncles had one or two children, or none. In 2001, Italy had zero growth. I believe Mussolini was giving money for any child born at that time. My parents never applied for such a thing, of course.

Our home was immaculate. Mother was meticulously cleaning and treating the different floors with polish. It had three bedrooms, a kitchen and a bath. The front entrance had an enclosed porch where we left our shoes. We never wore shoes inside. After this porch we came to a hallway lined by bedrooms, bathroom and a storage room. The kitchen was located at the end of the hallway. The hall and kitchen had marble floors, while the bedrooms had parquet floors. There was a larger bedroom for our parents, one for our two brothers, and one for us two girls. Marble floors are very common in Italy as well as tiles.

At the entrance of the hallway were many *pattini*, skates, pads that my mother made of thick material, usually from old wool coats, to fit our feet. She stitched several layers of material together into one inch thick pad. We always left our shoes on the covered porch and stepped into our skates. Then we could easily slide on the polished floors. This was a way of life and we thought it was fun and good. All the children that would visit our home had to do the same thing. In the summer, we were barefooted outside, and it was easier for us not having laces to untie. Our shoes were not ever to step on the polished floors.

Everything happened in the kitchen. When I was three or four years old, time seemed to stand still and life was nice and happy. My father went to work at the shipyard foundry, came home, and in his spare time, would build rabbit cages and goat sheds. Mother would have dinner ready as soon as my father came in. She would instruct us to remain quiet and good because Papa was tired. Mother was an extraordinary cook and everything tasted simply special. When we were growing up, even during the war, we had a very nutritious diet, mostly from our garden and animals.

We always had a vegetable garden, chickens, and rabbits. My mother's sole purpose was to take care of her family in the best way possible, with good food as well as a pleasant clean house. I don't remember ever eating candy until I was about ten years old and the American soldiers gave us candy and gum. Candy was certainly not a daily addition to our meals as it is often in American families. On holidays, we had homemade desserts such as strudel, *oresniaza,* or *potiza,* a dialect word for a pastry made of nuts.

My two older brothers would help with the chores while my sister and I played. There were rabbit cages to clean out and feeding all the animals. All the animals would be gathered for the night in their respective buildings. We herded chickens up the stairs to their roost, and goats to their houses, providing them with water for the night. All the animals were put away safely.

My aunt Irene would come to visit a few times a year from Milano. She brought us all the good things we otherwise would never see: dolls, toys, little undies, shirts. She lived in the big city of Milano during our childhood years, and she was glamorous to us, dressed in style, something we didn't see ordinarily. I knew my mother had been like that too when she was younger. I had seen pictures of her, beautifully dressed in the style of the day. Again, time stood still for a little while, then it disappeared from the memory, and my mother was just a housewife who had a very simple homemade dress.

War broke out and all the dreams were shattered. Life was full of these vanishing dreams. I witnessed them as they continued on their course of what appeared never-ending tragedies and losses.

4
The Simple Life

Our life was centered around the family and all our activities. Father had to milk the goats and he just knew so much more about farming than my mother. I always sensed that my mother was adjusting to all this farmwork. In her younger years she had been a well-dressed *commessa* or shop clerk. Father could do everything, even butchering, a job he did not like. At these times, he would become silent and thoughtful, and did not want anybody around. He used the area behind the stalls to skin the rabbits and spread their fur on boards. He had studied how to do the tanning. I remember many furs ready to use but I never had a coat made of fur. I think my mother simply did not know how to go about it.

My parents worked together for the good of the family, to provide for the cold winters and lack of fresh vegetables. Sometimes, winters were very long and cold, with the heavy winds (Bora) and rain when we would not go out of the house. The Bora could easily pick up children even when holding on to the ropes in the streets.

My father learned many of his farming skills from his own mother. She was from a family in Monte Nero (Crni Vrh) where processes were passed on, similar to the pioneers that canned everything. When I visited this area later in life, the old houses were still intact, their large gardens thriving with vegetables. I could imagine how he did the same sort of things with his mother, working together, preserving foods for the winters.

We had a colorful neighborhood, but I believed then that we were different than all the other families. In the group of families there, we were the only ones that had a large garden of vegetables and animals. There were even different customs within each family. This made a rare breed of people, which were only truly Fiumani. Then in Trieste, they are truly Triestini with certain traits, like quicker in speech and action. Mother said, "Vera Triestina," which she meant to be quick and shrewd.

The professor who lived adjacent to our home and garden, his wife, their daughter, Ornella, were completely isolated, it appeared to me. Ornella was slightly older than me. I never saw her mother and maybe once I saw the father. Their garden, in contrast to ours, was all roses, bushes, and trees, a fairy-tale garden. In our garden, only vegetables were growing and one large Empress tree near the alley dividing our house and garden. Under this tree, all our animals were housed in appropriate little buildings my father built. The garden was all enclosed with a wire fence. Wood fences were never seen in Italy. Across the narrow alley, our home or unit had a little cement walk all around to the front door. In between the walk and the house it was covered with geraniums, asters, zinnia, roses which made a colorful sight. Special herbs were everywhere and much used. Father would often make a sage tea, reputed to be good for colds, chest congestion, and sore throat.

We had so much—a nice home, big vegetable garden and so many animals. Every spring, there were new goats, new chicks, new rabbits, and a variety of hens. It was exciting when my father would come in early in the morning, all excited announcing two new kids. We'd run to see the new babies, they were barely able to stand up.

I can still see when my father was teaching my mother

how to prune roses, speaking in a soft voice. He was very patient and tolerant of her ignorance. His childhood had been very different with his own capable mother, teaching him gardening and canning, and later worked together on the family business when his father died.

We had Leghorns for eggs and the red chickens for meat. There were white and black speckled hens and bantams. It was fun to have different species and colors of chickens. We also had ducks and geese and they would be all free in the little courtyard which was fenced off from the vegetable garden. My father had a special ambition to get very different kinds of hens and other animals. We had Angora rabbits; long ears, different colors; brown, white and black rabbits. The rabbits were all in different cages according to their breed. Mother never did utilize the Angora wool, she just didn't know how to take it from the rabbits, or maybe it is combed out.

The goats were the most fun and most intelligent. We never had pigs. The goats had to be taken to pasture wherever there was grass and edible bushes. We had nothing for goats in our garden. The vegetables left over were given to the rabbits. Both animals loved hard old bread. Sometimes I was assigned to take the goats to pasture, and sometimes Sergio was. I had to hold on to their harnesses while they moved about, feeding on the hillside around Fiume. I loved my job and being out in the fields, but sometimes it was a little lonely with no one around. I was all by myself, following them holding as they pulled on the rope. I kept the thick rope close and watched them eat. While they were making little contented "Behh, behh" sounds. They would lead me where they wanted to go, I just followed them as they pulled the rope. I loved the smell of the earth, and the countryside with patches of dry grass. I sat on a rock and would look around the hills and little valleys. In the summer, it could be very dry, but we could find leafy pastures, which they really liked. The air could be hot, but there was always a breeze coming up from the Adriatic. It was not boring, it was a job somebody had to do.

Earlier, I had tagged along with Sergio. As we became bigger and older, the harder jobs were for the two older brothers, and easier jobs like pasturing fell to me. My sister, two years younger, did not have any jobs yet. I knew that Pippi and Sergio would do any job assigned to them and more. We were all working for the family. There was no other more important goal than this, except school, of course.

The goat milk was very strong tasting and I never liked it, but it was used in cooking. Nothing was ever wasted, everything was used. It had a strong odor that I just simply could not bring myself to drink. My father usually milked the goats as he knew more about farming than my mother. In fact, I always knew that my father could do anything in this world.

Father and Mother worked together to make sauerkraut in barrels. I watched my father, teaching my mother how the process needed to be done. He would patiently start: one layer of thinly sliced cabbage, then salt, then again layers of cabbage in an orderly fashion to keep it flat. Finally, when this process is done, one covers the top of the crock with a fine net, then a heavy wood lid that he made for this purpose with a large stone on top to crush down the cabbage. Turnips were preserved the same way. What was left of any vegetables would be taken to the rabbits. There were no such things as pellets or prepared food.

Fiume was a very warm memory. I remember well all the special streets and picturesque landscapes. After the war, several years later, away from Fiume, living in Florence, I longed to return to my native city and live again the wonderful life. But it was only a dream to nourish my fragmented childhood after the war. The dream vanished and I was in a new life.

5
Neighborhood

Besides our beautiful home, we had a large garden full of wonder. The chicken coops had little steps for the birds to climb up high to the off-the-ground dwelling. Every night, their doors and windows would be shot, the chickens perched on the pole across the coup. In the morning, my father would open them up before going off to work. My mother later would feed them and collect the eggs. The goat sheds were large enough for my sister and I to use as playhouses when the goats were outside. My father cleaned them very often. He liked the animals to be in clean sheds. We could pull pods from the tall pea vines and eat the young sweet peas. We would pull bright red radishes and carrots from the ground.

 There was an interesting family that lived across the courtyard from us. There were eight or nine children, which was an unusually large number for that time and place. The oldest girl, Aurelia, was about eighteen and would come often to visit my mother. She was always coughing and was very thin with stooped shoulders. You could see her bones from under her light cotton dresses. My mother would fix fresh eggs for her, or *zabaglione*. She would break two fresh eggs from our chickens into a bowl, blend with sugar using a spoon as an eggbeater, to make a creamy sweet pudding. She also fixed other healthy food for her. While she was doing this, she would keep my sister and I occupied so we wouldn't be underfoot while she and Aurelia were visiting. Mother was very tender and warm to the girl as they visited. They spend good times together. After Aurelia went home, I would see her with tears in her eyes. She was worried about the young girl and the family. I knew she felt helpless and unable to do more. The destiny of so many children and little income, was well underway with the current of life. Even my mother could not intervene.

Eventually, I learned that this girl was neglected by her family and had advanced tuberculosis. Her father was often drunk when he came home, and her mother was always busy with a new baby. Their house was rundown and at dusk I saw the cockroaches coming out of their house. Their home was infested with the bugs and the house also had a very old bad odor, unlike our clean smell we were accustomed to. I could smell that odor from the street outside.

I felt very sad for all those children, they did not look happy. They always played by themselves as the other neighbor kids stayed away. I made a big effort to remember their names, but today I can only think of Aurelia, a fragile girl with long brown hair, deep sad eyes.

Our own family of four was considered to be large, but the family across from us was past all reasonable limits. There was another family that had many children in the complex, but they all looked well fed. I heard some people talk about Aurelia's family, "They want to please Mussolini and get extra money for each new baby!" One time, I heard my mother say: "Oh! Oh! He is coming home drunk again! Another baby will be on the way." This was only said about Aurelia's family.

I loved that neighborhood and was happy there. Then the war started and we had to run to the shelters with airplanes flying overhead. A few times, I saw the bombs shining in the air whistling as they came down. My brother would try to reassure us, saying they were not aimed at us or our houses. I heard the talk that our parents and my older brother would have after the bombing. They said if areas near home were hit, it was only a mistake. A target misjudgement. It was not meant for that area. My father said it is difficult to judge and aim just right. I knew that the discussions were with a feeling of forgiveness and acceptance, and not of blame.

It was not very pleasant in the shelters, so we would run home after the curfew. Many times we had to run again shortly after getting home because of another air raid. My brother carried my little sister on his shoulders and pulled me along. I was scared and shaky until we got to the shelter entrance under the sheer rock face. Then we descended gradually into the long corridors underground. It was like going into a mine only these tunnels did not need roof support because they were carved in solid rock and were also made larger and taller. These tunnels would go right through, across the mountain, opening to the other side of the hill. There were two entrances. Here, we were safe from the bombs, but it was very disturbing when there was an explosion close enough so my ears would feel the rush of air through the tunnel. I would cover my ears as soon as I could, but my ears would still hurt.

It was very important to find a good location in the crowded space in the tunnel where we could spread out blankets and set up folding chairs. We had to stay there several hours sometimes. The sirens would signal the end of the attack. My mother would not let us stay there any longer than required because she felt the shelter was too damp and unhealthy with so many people crowded together. Often, we didn't get in fast enough to get a good place, so we had to sit on the damp floor.

Sometimes when the sirens would sound, my mother

would not be able to keep up with us during our run to the entrance. When she was a small girl in Budapest, she had been injured. She had a difficult time with her left leg, which was fused at the knee. We waited at the shelter entrance and we were happy when we saw her come limping in. Sometimes she would not be there and then I became very apprehensive. After Sergio's death, I was afraid she didn't care enough to run from danger. Then after the curfew, I would run home, and only after seeing her I could breathe normally and quiet down my apprehension. I remained very fearful for my mother and I was always very close by her. Later, I would not let her go anywhere alone. Children may be able to perceive more than we give credit.

6
Special Holidays

In the cold, wintry December, when the days become short and dark, small children stay inside the house safe and warm. At this time of year in Fiume and Trieste, there is often a strong wind called Bora that is almost like a little tornado and is very cold. The sound of the wind is very alarming and eerie. But on a certain day in December, the children know that a very old woman, with a cane, all dressed in a long black dress will be roaming the streets.

Mothers admonish children to be good. My mother said, "If you will be good, you will get some toys. If you are bad, you will only get a sack of coal." Mother, a stranger from another country, followed all the customs of Italy with us children.

On that night, I spied from the window to see if I could see *La Befana*, the old woman. One time I thought I did see her, before I ran to hide. She was all bent over with a sack of toys sticking out of the bag that was on one shoulder. On the other shoulder she had a smaller sack, all black. It was exciting and we could hardly go to sleep that night.

Next morning, I went outside the door to look for the gift from *La Befana*. She was always good to us and we never found coals. *La Befana* was indeed a very good grandmother and I knew she loved children.

The next event was preparation for Christmas. For this we had to scrounge all over the hills and woods for the much sought *muschio* for the *presepio*, which is the nativity scene. We tried to gather as much *muschio*, or moss, as we could, then at home we would prepare a table for the scene. We placed carefully all the moss to resemble hills where Jesus lived long ago. Then we placed little figurines, the manger and the animals, sheep, donkeys, camels, and we had only one or two shepherds. This nativity scene was in every house and I am sure nobody had a Xmas tree, because I never saw one. There were no presents because the presents were only brought by *La Befana*. This family holiday was very peaceful and happy. Mother would make many sweet cakes, cookies, and always the rolled up walnut pastry that was typical for this season. This we called *oresniaza*. I'm sure it's a dialect word that only that part of Italy would recognize. It was not easy. I helped by mincing the walnuts very finely. It is done similarly to the strudel, which is with apples. She did both of these pastries, and many cookies.

Our family was a little different because we were not Catholic. So this was a special time for us. Other Italians have many more holidays, especially with their patron saints. Our parents did not believe in all this, we were Protestant. They even gave us names that did not have a patron saint: Ireneo, Sergio, Leda, and Vilma.

As different as we were, I never wished to be Catholic with all the rituals and the ornate churches. Our Valdensian church was very simple with only benches and a pulpit. No saints on the walls and no statues. Our pastor had only a black tunic which he wore only during the service, then he would be in regular clothes talking softly to all the people. I loved going to our church.

New Years Eve was another event for us. We were armed with pot lids and at midnight we would all go outside and bang the lids together making a lot of noise. There was noise all over, because everybody was doing the same thing. I knew that this was all to bring in the New Year and be happy.

Our cheer and fun, however, ended before I was six years old. These happy occasions became only a fading memory.

7
World War I

All the qualified men of the region had to be enlisted in the Austro-Hungarian Army. This region was Eastern Italy and Slovenia, including Fiume (Rijeka) where Paolo and Philip, (Lippi as he was called) lived as young men. An old picture shows the two men I recognize, my father and Uncle Paolo. They were comrades in this war. They visited each other's homes.

Philip, my father, grew up in the area of Slovenia and later Fiume. He grew up with a close-knit family of very religious people. When he was a young boy, he was the altar boy in their Catholic church.

This family grew up closely together, working along with their mother doing all the chores, such as taking care of the horses and other animals, preserving food for the winter and even making Slivovitz with the abundance of plums in their lot. The many relations on both sides of the Stegel/Premeru (maiden name) family often would have festivities together, where the men were sure to have a glass of the potent Slivovitz.

As a young man, Philip was popular, a good dancer, agile in the local traditional dances, and he also had a good voice that could lead all the party in wonderful evenings of singing native Slovenian songs, as well as opera arias.

His older sister, Zinka, had many hopes for him and was proud of him, being the man of the family now that their father was gone. She had lined up many acceptable young girls, usually from a good family, to marry.

In contrast, Uncle Paolo grew up as a stranger in a country where he came as a young child, from Hungary. His own mother could never speak the language of his contemporaries. This large family was not well to do and they had some obscure tragedies with at least two children. The family had only each other and no other relations. All the children able to work had to do so, for the family without a father.

Philip's family was not happy when he made good friends with Paolo's sisters and brother. Eventually, my mother, Yolanda charmed Philip and they were married. She was not from the desirable family that was hoped for, and not a Catholic, the last being the worst for a devout family. For a few years, there was a little distance between the two differing families, especially with Aunt Zinka. She was really the head of the family as she was smart, skillful, but opinionated, and with no tolerance for infidels, as she called anyone not Catholic. She was a strong influence in the family. This was well hidden for the most part, and growing up, we were not aware, except with a child's perception. I sensed that my father's sister felt she had little in common with us. While Nonna Stegel visited us for several days often on from Split, *Zia Zinka* came to the border with Nada and Zivko, her children, only for a very short visit at the iron gate. Either she did not have the stamp to enter Italy from Yugoslavia, or did not plan to come visit us at our home. Later in life, we all became very good friends, but then I was here in the USA. We wrote many letters to each other, finally getting to know each other.

My father's mother was all the family we needed and wanted. Nonna Stegel, much different than Nonna Soltesz, (my mother's mother) could speak perfect Italian and most of all our familiar dialect. She loved us so much, she played with us and she was a perfect grandmother. Her expression just told me she loved to be with us. Her hair in a bun, white as snow, her roundish figure under her all black skirts, invited lots of hugs and she hugged back with sweet kisses on our cheeks. She made up for everything.

8
Ornella

Our garden was a magical world for me. I was in awe and I loved the big Empress tree which was at least thirty feet high. It was majestic, with purple flowers in spring. Year round, it had large tropical leaves, although now I know this tree is deciduous. In my memory, I never saw it bare. This tree was truly majestic and when it was blooming season, it became completely purple with the exotic flowers. It dominated a large corner of the garden where all the goats, chickens and rabbits houses were situated.

A little further over, there was the open areas of the vegetable garden. It flourished, with tall bean stalks, peas and all the low vegetables, lettuce, and green peppers. The root vegetables were also divided in sections for beets, potatoes, radishes, and turnips.

I remember two neighbors that made an impression on my five-year-old mind. The two-story brick apartment complex where we lived had another building just like it on the other side of a little courtyard. We were at the end and bottom floor of the first complex. Across the courtyard began the other brick building with the same amount of units. One neighbor was across from the courtyard and up one story. This was a big family. We lived on the main floor of the brick complex on the other side of the courtyard. Part of the bargain for living on the bottom floor was we could have a piece of land. I am sure when our family first moved there, they chose this corner dwelling for that reason. I am also sure there was nothing but rubble or at least wild area where now our garden was full of vegetables. Father no doubt transformed it into a lush area.

The other neighbor was adjacent to us with their garden alongside ours. This was a very small family. Their garden next to ours was an enchanted area for me. This garden did not have vegetables, but it was like a tropical jungle that we could barely see through. The fragrance of roses and flowers drifted into our yard, from their isolated world. It was so quiet there and even scary at times. I never heard any sounds, only the rustling of leaves and bushes. I really never could see anyone there, but could hear some motion and could sense a presence, like when one feels a ghost.

Sometimes, I sensed the presence of a girl of about six or seven in the garden and caught the glimpse of her apron. I knew this family had a little girl and I knew her name was Ornella. She was already going to school while I was not yet old enough. She was the only child of these reclusive neighbors. I never saw them outside, and the father must have left early in the morning for work. Their entrance was hidden from our house. Their porch, like ours, was enclosed completely with the vines of the wisteria (glicini).

I would spy through the branches, but I really could not see through the trees and thick vegetation. I wanted to talk to her, but even when I made a sound, she would not answer. She must have not had permission to talk to us. This little family was very private and isolated.

Our own family was not one to mix around with the others in the same complex. My parents were just too busy and kept to themselves. But at least we had a lot of coming and going between house and garden. I don't think my mother even knew the names of the people living in the complex because she had nicknames for different people. One was *La Grassa,* another *Gambe di Spaghetti,* and the

Germans were *gnocchi*, because they were thick-headed. The worst would have been: *Testa de Capuzo*, dialect for someone not too bright.

One day all life disappeared from the magical garden. After several days, I realized that the house and garden were abandoned. The family was gone. The garden was silent, no more little footsteps.

The mystery was never solved for me. For a long time, I went near their garden to listen, but I could not hear the hesitant little steps on the leaves on the ground, trying to hide their presence. I could not hear someone brushing against the bushes or even the unmistakable feeling of a presence there, even if I could not see.

Something must have happened and I felt sad and even lonely, like I had lost a friend. For a long time, I could see the ghost of a girl walking through her garden and I could smell the fragrances drifting with a little breeze as if the rose bushes were beings touched by a little girl's hands, but all life had gone forever.

That was the start of the war years, where Germans were always marching all over town, as if to impress their power. They seemed to be everywhere, looking for all kinds of people to take as prisoners of war. They would come in small little platoons of four or six, or even twos, but they always marched it seemed to me. They did not walk normally, in a relaxed manner. They had very noisy boots that clicked on the sidewalks. Most people were unaware at this point of what was going on and I only had a child's instinct. I dreaded seeing Germans and I was afraid of them. They had rifles across their shoulders, guns at their waist, and belts of bullets. The German soldiers always looked taller than other people, even my father, who was at least six feet. Their impressive uniforms and all the guns and boots, made them so much bigger. Even our Italian *Bersaglieri* and *Alpini* were not as imposing.

The garden remained silent and it was no longer fun, but only very sad.

9
Happy Childhood Then a Fading Dream

Our kitchen was a gathering place. Here, we all ate together, our family of four children, while my mother served Hungarian food. She preferred to cook Hungarian dishes rather than Italian. She was a very patriotic Hungarian in every way. She never spoke the Italian language perfectly, she transposed some words, and had her own particular syntax. I only knew she did not talk as other Italians, with the same accent. This fact made her even more singularly special to me.

The kitchen was also a meeting place for my father's friends and coworkers. We children would not come in and out of the kitchen. They did not need to tell us this, we just knew. The kitchen door was closed and discussion of politics were going on very seriously. All the men had their say, and my father was one of the leaders for the cause. I heard always with my third ear. I could hear his strong voice often, talking about *giustizia sociale*. I was really tuned in even in my play, out in the hall! We did not have a radio, but I had seen people putting their ears to a radio in other homes listening for the news. Now these men were discussing what they heard on the radio. My mother served them *palacinche*, a sort of *crépe suzette*, and wine. She never had to come out to admonish us about being loud or disturbing. We children knew what was expected, and I don't remember my mother ever scolding us or having to explain. Actually, they were a lot louder in the kitchen, now and then with a crescendo of voices, then down to one voice.

The talk was about imminent war and all the injustices about the fascist regime and the Germans. It sounded disturbing and I was apprehensive when these meetings took place. I had seen the Germans in their impressive uniforms, in big groups marching in the streets, their boots making a roar in my ears. The fascists were also marching a lot, with their round caps with the bouncing tassels, and shining black knee boots.

A group of little girls were playing in the hallway. My sister and I and two other four-year-olds. The hall was close to the kitchen. We were playing quietly, probably because we wanted to listen in. My older brother, Ireneo, we called him Pippi, was often with them too, mostly listening. My younger brother, Sergio was usually out busy with his wanderings around the neighborhood or countryside.

During my childhood, I remember playing games as kids in other countries do: a group of little girls holding hands and going around and around singing: "Giro, giro tondo, casca il mondo, casca la tera, a tutti per tera . . ." (in dialect) and we would all fall down. When we were outside, with bigger groups, we would form a large circle holding hands, then singing the game: "*O quanti figli avete, madama do re?*" One half of the group would answer and step inside the circle. This game had definite steps and it was for older girls. I was not usually included, I would just watch.

There was also a performing time where the bravest of girls would sing a song in front of the other children. There were special songs that everybody knew like "*Mamma*" and "*La Via del bosco*" and so many more that now I remember only when I hear them. Luciano Pavarotti has sung many of these old songs.

My Aunt Irene, for whom my brother Ireneo was named, would come and visit a few times a year from Milano. She always brought gifts, bought with her small savings, just for us. She had a very simple job and very little money, which she saved just for gifts for us. Mostly it was clothes, but one time, she brought beautiful dolls for my sister and me. I was always tightly clutching this doll in my arms, so that nobody could take it away from me. We would never have had any of these nice things if it weren't for my Aunt Irene. My sister and I were the little girls she never had. My mother was in her forties when my sister and I were born. She had many worries and not much patience. She was worried about my seventeen-year-old brother because he was nearing the age when he was subject to be drafted into the army. Aunt Irene was a big support to my mother. The two sisters were very close.

Many thoughts were going through my mother's mind. For my brother to join the fascist army was not really a choice. Our family was never pro-Duce even though the whole country followed Mussolini. The other kids in the neighborhood joined the youth groups: *Balilla* and *Figli della Lupa.* We were not part of it. Sometimes I was jealous, thinking, *Why can't I also wear these pretty uniforms and go to special marching events?*

Before the war, it seemed as though everybody was a fascist. Then, after the war, it appeared that nobody wanted to admit this openly.

There was a feeling of uneasiness and after meetings at our house, even the usual accordion music did not lighten up the men's faces. Somebody in the group always brought their accordion to play after a while and then include the children in the fun and songs. In every crowd in Italy, there was always someone who could play and all would join in to sing the old songs.

Even then, I had a feeling that life as I had known in my short life was coming near an end. Children are tuned in so well to their surroundings, and may have a deeper feeling even than adults. Yes, I knew our beautiful life was coming to an end. The first tragedy hit our family sooner than we realized.

10

Sergio, My Brother

He was a boy of ten, blue eyes, sun-streaked blond hair, lean but strong and athletic, with a temperament of an outgoing, truly giving child. He was always ready for any chores or requests from my mother. We were a beautiful family of four children, two boys and two girls. I was preschool age, but I remember my brother well.

Sergio could always make my mother smile, with a little joke or a tease, since her face was serious most of the time. I could see her smile when Sergio talked to her, she even laughed at times. He was a consolation to her; he understood her worries and made light of any subject he could, even showed bugs to her that he had captured. He was also a great storyteller, telling tall stories, of course. The two had a special relationship, as if he was making every moment precious for her. Was it because there wouldn't be too many more? It is strange how some people know so much before it really happens.

Sergio would never come home empty-handed from his excursions. It might be just a few apples or a handful of nails, even some pieces of wood that looked good to him. Everything would come home for some future use.

My father was very organized with his tools and his supplies to work with (nails, etc.). He had a little cubicle room on the porch where he kept all his valuable tools, nails, screws. He always had a tool for the job and I remember he valued every little tool, whether it was just a hole puncher or a drill. Whatever Sergio brought home, it was appreciated and stored in neat order according to their future use. Big nails in one box, screws in another, all according to size. The tools were usually hanging on the wall.

One day in late summer, Sergio was gone on his usual adventurous trips around the countryside. He was always very busy with friends or alone roaming about when he was not needed at home. Usually, I did not pay attention to him as I played with dolls, rearranging dolls furniture, and dressing dolls.

Then one dark day came when the world collapsed for us. It was September 1940. I was five years old. I remember vividly all the details of those days.

11

The Boots

Everything was going fine for my mother till she saw his boots. She had been waiting for him, now she finally saw him coming home. Mother had been worried about him.

He was an average size boy of ten or eleven, lean with blue eyes and wavy blond hair, his intelligence showing in all his features. He had a perfectly shaped boy's head, and his facial expression showed alertness and passion in all his movements. He loved his life, his family and his adventures. I remember him in Tirolean-style short pants and a white shirt. His arms, and legs were browned by the sun at the end of summer. His cheeks, always bronzed and flushed with excitement, were now pale.

He was my brother.

This day, Sergio was gone on his usual adventurous trips around the countryside. He could travel well with his wornout boots. On this particular day, he came home with hands full of ripe figs to give to Mother. He would never come home empty-handed. He always had treasures to bring to his family, either some trinkets for us girls, his little sisters, or something he thought would be useful for my father or mother.

On this warm late summer day, he went past me, limping. His bleached eyebrows were in a frown and his blue eyes were troubled with anxiety. He went to Mother and I ran behind him.

After looking closely, mother saw his wornout ankle

boots had streaks of dry blood and his left knee was dirty and mixed with blood. He had a deep wound on his knee.

He was talking to mother: "I wanted to get some ripe figs to bring home."

"Where was this?" Mother interrupted.

"A long ways from here. I have been walking home for one hour or more but the knee really hurts and I could not walk faster."

So Sergio had walked limping while his wound bled. Seeing him with his knee bleeding frightened me. He was in pain, I could see it in his face, but he did not complain or cry. I had a deep feeling of a sad omen. Anxiety was churning in my stomach. The fragrances of late summer of mixed flowers and ripe pears and apples permeating from the garden did not comfort me, as these were the fragrances of our safe home.

Mother called out to my older brother Ireneo, or Pippi, as we called him as children. "*Presto,* right way, go get Papa at work." He was working at *Cantieri Navali,* just below our house.

She was visibly shaken by this accident. She tried not to show her concern and not alarm me, as I was watching the whole scene intently.

Sergio continued his story of what had happened.

"The fruit was high up on the tree. I climbed up, then the branch broke and I fell on some rocks under the tree. There were mules and cows tied to the tree." The area had droppings from the animals.

My father came quickly, as the foundry where he worked was close to our house, which overlooked the port and shipping yard on the outskirts of the city.

My fourteen-year-old brother and my father formed a portable chair with their arms crossed. Mother lifted Sergio on the make-do sitting gurney and they started running to the hospital, which entailed taking a little train to get into the city. Mother followed them.

I waited at home for Sergio to come back from the hospital. He returned the next day and Mother settled him in a chair on the porch propping his legs on another chair.

Something had changed about Sergio. He was quiet, drawing pictures with colored pencils. He kept busy and did not talk much. Every day, my mother bought him out on the porch, cool with the surrounding wisteria. Here, my brother created wonderful art for Mother. The drawing revealed beautiful gardens with myriad of flowers with blue skies. He was so peaceful and serene now, not in pain, and not anxious to go somewhere to explore. He was calm and so good to me, calling me to see the drawings. Asking, "Do you like them?"

Then one last drawing I remember was of a cemetery with many white crosses and past them, crosses vanishing, giving way to a bluest sky beyond. The scene opened to a beautiful land of trees, flowers and bright light. I could not help saying, *"Il paradiso!"*

I realized later that Sergio was preparing Mother for the trip he would take to a world of incomparable beauty, and he wanted her to know that.

The dark day came when the world collapsed for us. Sergio was gone. They had to take him again to the hospital where doctors admonished my mother to let him go in peace. They did not let her see him in his last throes of the tetanus. All attempts to save him were in vain and Sergio died within a few days. I heard people and Mother saying often: *"In pace."* They had to let him in go in peace.

Our wonderful family of four children now was lost without the enthusiasm and love of Sergio.

He was gone and my mother lost a big part of herself with him. The child that had brought so much love and understanding was gone. My mother was never the same after this. Her black clothes were all she would wear from then on.

Sergio knew that he was dying, and during the few days at home, he prepared my mother as best as he could. The pictures of bright light and ethereal countryside were for her and at last, he told her not to worry. He was going to be in such beautiful places and he would be happy in the hillside of trees and flowers. I was five years old, and I remember my dearest brother in a child *bara* (coffin) all dressed in white and he was beautiful, a sleeping angel. Tears would not stop from my eyes, and I was walking around like a shadow, not talking at all, hiding in corners, hiding from the world that collapsed around me.

12

The Letter

To my fourteen-year-old brother, Ireneo, fell the responsibility to inform the family on my father's side of what had happened. My mother's family were all in Fiume, but Father's family was in Split, Croatia.

The translation of his letter:

Fiume 23 Ottobre, 1940
My dearest Zia Zinka,
  With immense pain, we inform you of the death of our dear Sergio, which happened on 25 September at 10 in the evening.
  Mamma and Papa are so sad and in such a pain they cannot write, not even to Nonna, because they are afraid she will suffer and become ill.
  For this reason, I write to you. The 16th of September was the fatal day. Sergio fell from a fig tree and suffered a wound under the knee. Papa had taken him right away to the hospital, where they applied three stitches. Eight days, he was well, and then suddenly he became very ill and his condition worsened and tetanus developed. He was taken again to the hospital with the ambulance, where after two days and two nights, with atrocious suffering, he died. On the 27th of September, there was a funeral which was beautiful.
  There were many children and boys, his friends, with their families. There was a chorus of boys that sang the *Miserere*. There were many many friends and among them, Signora Prade and other of your friends.

Nonna Soltesz cries so much and she cannot console herself, and just yesterday she went to live with Zio Paolo, (she lived with our family a few years) because here everything reminds her of Sergio, whom she loved so much.

I wrote to you all that I know, maybe some day Papa will decide to write a little better to Nonna Stegel.

Sergio is a little angel who will pray for all of us.

Here, I attach a copy of the service that our pastor had at the cemetery.

I send greetings to you in the name of all of us.

—-Boris
(as he was called by that side of the family in Croatia.)

Fiume 23 X 1940

Mia carissima Zia Zinka,
Con immenso dolore Ti annunciamo la morte del nostro Caro Sergio.
Che e avvenuta il 25 di Settembre alle 10 di sera.

La mamma e papa' sono tanto addolorati che non possono scrivere neanche alla nonna, perche hanno paura che Le fara male.

Per questo Ti scrivo a Te; il 16 Settembre il giorno fatale, Sergio e cascato da un albero di fico, ha fatto una ferita sotto il ginocchio; papa' lo ha portato subito all'ospedale dove gli hanno fatto tre punti; otto giorni stava bene, ed in una volta il male si aggravo' e suberntro il tetano, venne portato con l'aubulanza all'ospedale di nuovo, dove, dopo due giorni e due notti con atroci sofferenze moriva. Gli furono fatto il funerale che riusci assai bello.

Intervennero molti bambini e ragazzi, suoi amici colle famiglie, il coro dei ragazzi hanno cantato il Miserere, e molti conoscenti fra i quali anche la signora Prade e tanti vostri conoscenti. La nonna Soltesz tanto piange e non si puo consolare, e giusto ieri e andata ad abitare da zio Paolo perche qui tutto Le ricorda Sergio che gli voleva tanto bene.

Io Ti ho scritto tutto quello che sapevo, un giorno si decidera forse anche papa' a scrivere meglio alla Nonna.

Sergio e un angioletto che pregara per noi tutti; qui Ti aggiungo una copia del culto che il nostro Pastore ha tenuto al cimitero.

Saluto in nome di tutti noi, voi tutti.

—Boris

(Written as a boy of fourteen, with some dialect words and punctuation problems.)

13

The Loss

My mother never seemed to recover from the loss of Sergio. It was such a tragic death . . . and so sudden! He was only ill for a few days after the accident. The wound was taken care of in the hospital, but when tetanus attacked his system, we were helpless to do anything.

My mother made an enlarged picture of Sergio and kept it on her bedroom dresser. Her eyes were dark and deep set. She was always secretly crying. I went along with her, in her daily shopping through the streets. I saw her studying boys of the same age as Sergio. She was in some way in denial of his death.

There was one incident, I remember well, that it revealed that she could not console herself. One day, she came home with a boy who actually looked like Sergio. I studied this boy and his features, staring at his expressions and his manners. He was very close, but I knew he could never be Sergio. Sergio had love pouring out of his being, this boy was harsher in his manner.

Mother had found this boy just playing in the streets and asked his parents if he could spend some time with our family. I had a feeling that his parents happily approved of this arrangement. He was not from a well-to-do family, or at least a family like ours. He did not have manners and was not even polite.

I don't remember the name of the boy, but I know my mother looked at him trying to see Sergio. He stayed with us a few days, but it soon became apparent that he was not the innocent Sergio who was full of love for everyone and tender with animals and even insects. This boy was wise in the ways of the world, was not kind to our animals, and not to us girls either. He deceived my mother and he would act one way with her, then take advantage of her depressed condition, even stealing.

After a short time, he was gone. Either he left, which I believe really happened, or my mother could have taken him back home. He was gone as suddenly as he came.

After this short uplift, my mother again plunged in deep despair. She was always quiet and sad. One time, I found out that after putting us to bed she would walk to the cemetery in the dark and spend a good part of the night there on Sergio's grave. When winter came, I was very worried and afraid that she would be found frozen on the tomb. Winter in Fiume can be very cold, with a strong wind, the Bora. A few times, I walked to the cemetery, fighting my own fear, and convinced her to come back home.

Then the war started, and more sadness was to come our way.

14

The Good Life

When one is born into a family that is nurturing and values the needs of the children above anything else, one is very rich. Ours was such a family.

As far back as I remember, my father worked long hours in the shipyard. After work, he came home and worked in the vegetable garden, then he also cleaned out the rabbit cages and chicken coops. My mother had our meals on the table at a regular hour and these meals were wonderful and nutritious. Only a mother's cooking can be like that. She used all the vegetables from our garden, and for meat, we had chicken and rabbit. The goats were kept for milk only. I am certain I never ate goat meat. My parents were not farmers, but they believed in being self-sufficient. A single paycheck was not enough for a family of six that included four growing children, even in those days.

These memories were of my preschool years, before the war. Mother kept the house immaculate: we each had our own bed and children's furniture. My parents' bedroom had a mahogany set, which was very beautiful. Mother valued her furniture and I saw her polishing the wood with special oils. It always looked like new, with not a scratch or blemish. In Italy, houses come completely empty, no closets, no shelves or cabinets. All furniture was paid "a rate," or in monthly payments. Mother insisted on a better style of living than the other families around us. The master bedroom consisted of mahogany bed, an armoire, a dresser with a mirror, and chairs.

The children's bedrooms were of a lesser quality, with plain furniture. For us girls, it was white wood. It was the same for the kitchen, all white cabinets, marble table and wooden chairs.

My father built shelves in the bathroom and our small indoor storage room. This may not be a talent that many men in Italy may have even today. When I visited in later years, I found that people were inclined to call the *operaio* or the appropriate craftsman to repair or build anything. However, my two cousins in northern Italy, Ezio and Franco, are very handy do-it-yourself types and do their own repairs.

We were never allowed to walk into the house with shoes. Often, I would see Mother on her hands and knees washing the marble floors, and polishing the parquet floors in the bedrooms.

My older brother, Ireneo, was already an apprentice in the shipyard while my younger brother Sergio was always bringing home things that were useful in one way or another. He was only ten but already felt he had to contribute to the family. He would find pieces of wood, sections of chicken wire, bits and pieces that my father could utilize. He would also swipe apples or other fruit from distant orchards and bring home to eat or cook. Mother could make wonderful strudel. My sister Vilma, or Vilmetta as she was called, and I were cared for and loved by our brothers, always protecting us and talking to us like two little men. They never interfered with our games and friends. I don't remember any of us fighting or being disagreeable to each other. The job of reprimanding was for our parents. We all had some jobs to do, one of mine was collecting eggs sometimes with my mother.

Almost all our aunts and uncles lived in Fiume, except for Zia Irene and my father's sisters. When Aunt Irene would be coming to visit us, there would be a holiday atmosphere. She always stayed with our family because she was so close to my mother. We would be excited for days and there was a constant question: "When is Auntie coming?" Zia Irene was so much younger than my mother that she was more in tune with us kids. Mother was already in her forties when my sister and I were born.

All this happy life ended with the death of Sergio and then the war. Our beloved Sergietto was gone and our happy life was gone, it seemed, forever.

15

The Bombing

The air raids started and shelters were ready for us deep in the mountainous region where we lived.

From our house to the shelter was quite a little distance, maybe three blocks. After the entrance, there was the moderately steep descent into the tunnel, into the deep rock of the hillside. As we walked in, the path would become darker and darker until there was light only from our lanterns.

The tunnel enlarged about halfway down, into a natural cavern. Here was the greatest concentration of people. Some people would always either reach the shelter early or reserved the space. They'd stake out their spot, even taking turns in keeping it for their family or friends. Most people preferred the spot nearer the entrance, the air became very stuffy the further in. We usually had to walk further into the cavern to find a place to sit. Most people brought folding chairs, blankets, and most would just sit and wait, some people would lay down and cover their ears. When the bombing would start there were the compression waves, going through the tunnel. This was a very uncomfortable feeling especially in the ears. Sometimes, we had to be buried in there for three to four hours, but eventually the sirens would signal the end of the bombing. We could then go home. There were curfews that lasted the whole day because bombers came back many times at short intervals.

The shelters were damp and cold, so we had to wrap

ourselves in blankets for the long periods just waiting for the signal to come out. Occasionally, the sirens sounded too late, especially after we had just emerged from the shelter and returned to our homes. At these times, I would see the shiny, silver bombs dropping with a whistle all the way down from the airplanes. They were maybe aimed at the ships in the harbor. We were always reassured by Pippi, our brother, that they would not hit our home. I always had a feeling that these airplanes were really our friends, from the attitude of our family. As a child, I always seemed to assimilate what was going around me. I don't remember a lot of talking and explaining from our parents. The discussions of war were not shared with children.

Most of the city's homes, including ours, were on the hill overlooking the water and were generally out of danger. But one day, we came back from the shelter and were shocked to find that one of the bombs had landed in our yard. There was a big hole in the ground and our huge, majestic empress tree was lying on its side. The vegetable garden was totally destroyed and the animal pens were flattened. Our goats, rabbits, chickens and ducks were all dead. Our house was like a mouth of a cave. All our beautiful furniture was mostly smashed and all windows were broken. We had to dig through the rubble to salvage clothes and any other belongings we could find. I remember that only one cabinet and the singer sewing machine were almost intact, spared by a thick wall. All the fruits of our family's labor were destroyed.

16

My Father's Youth

My father was the oldest in his family of four children, two brothers, and two sisters. His father, whom I knew only as Nonno Stegel, was long gone when I was small, but I learned some important facts about him from my father. He had suffered a stroke one year, and a few years later suffered a second one and did not survive. He was still fairly young, most likely in his forties, when the first stroke left him paralyzed on his left side: his left arm useless, unable to use his hand. His left leg only useful for balance, being rigid and not completely flaccid. He had probably willed himself to walk again. This condition did not deter him from making a living for his family.

Nonno Stegel managed a drayage transport business in Fiume then, now Rijeka. At that time, early 1900s, that meant using draft horses and wagons. I heard many times the story of how he was able to manage these big horses with only one hand. Usually, four horses to a wagon were a handful for a healthy man. My father always described his father with amazement and respect. This extraordinary man was my grandfather. Even though I was very young, I remember thinking about this grandfather a lot. He must have had a strong will and resourcefulness; enough to want to continue to work at a job that required special skills and strength. These attributes were also instilled in my father.

My father, as the oldest, was the one to assist and then to take over the business when he was very young. He was only sixteen or seventeen when he had to assist with the drayage transport business. His father's second stroke, which killed him, left my father in charge of running the family business for a few years.

A fire in the barn just before WWI left all the horses perishing and wiped out the family income. By that time, however, most of the children were able to work outside the home and my father had to enlist in the Austro-Hungarian Army.

I know that my father was very close to his mother, whom I will always remember. The visits she often made to our home showed how much my father loved his mother. By this time, she lived with the only married daughter in Split. They always acted as if they were old friends, not just mother and son. They would talk at length in their native language, Slovenian, which sounded very sweet to me. Although I did not understand the language, I could see the respect and affection my father had for my wonderful, white-haired grandma, Nonna Stegel. After the death of my grandfather, she lived in Split, Croatia, with her two daughters, Zinka and Milka. Milka, the youngest, never married. Zinka had two children and became a widow when my two cousins were very young. Philip, my father, and Pepi, my uncle, were both in Fiume and married. A family now almost disappeared, like a dream. There is no Stegel to carry on that name.

My grandmother was always laughing and joking with us, playing simple children's games at which only children and grandmothers could have fun. She wore large gathered skirts. She would always have her white hair tied in a bun, her blue eyes sparkled with joy, and some mischief too. I would sit in her lap, she holding my hands, and then she would chant to me in Slovenian words I could not understand and she would point her head to the ceiling. As I would look up, she would open her legs and I would fall almost to the floor in her skirt.

Her hair was silky, completely white, her blue eyes twinkled and her sweet face was just beautiful to me. She was so much fun and so loving. She could communicate well with us in Italian, but all her games were in Slovenian and it was all that was needed for our children's games with her.

My father must have had a very happy childhood even with the difficulties, because his mother could always turn everything into joking. My father was like that in my early childhood, before the war.

Other Members of His Family

My father, Filippo, had a brother, Uncle Pepi, and two sisters—Aunt Zinka, and Aunt Milka. My father was always called Lippi, his brother Pepi, short for Giuseppe. Zia Zinka was very serious and well educated, while Milka was task-oriented and very quiet. All four were very close to the same age. The family lived in Fiume, until my Aunt Zinka married a banker, Zivko Rusic, who was transferred to Split in Croatia, several hundred miles down the coast from Fiume, on the Adriatic coast.

While Zio Pepi was a colorful, lively man, the younger sister, Milka, was quiet and shy. She never married. She was content to assume the role of housekeeper. She did the grocery shopping every day and cooked the meals. My father told me she had meningitis when she was little. Zia Milka had been protected during her growing years. She was comfortable with her tasks and helping raise Zia Zinka's two children. When Zia Zinka moved to Split, Milka followed, with Nonna.

Zia Zinka became a widow early on. Nonna Stegel passed on a few years later, not from illness, but from abdominal surgery and peritonitis. Nonna remained in Split for a few years and lived with the two daughters, and together raised Zinka's son, Zivko, and daughter, Nada. I thought both children were spoiled by the adults in their lives. Nonna, however, loved us so much, never showing any favoritism. I knew she was ours, too, but nevertheless I was a bit jealous of my cousins. Zia Zinka had met her husband while doing secretarial work in the bank. She resumed this work after her husband's death, while Milka stayed at home. I was only able to visit with them a few times while I was growing up. They would travel to Susak, the border town across the bridge from Fiume. We would just go to the gate and talk across the high railing, not very much as we did not speak each other language. Later in life, I became very close to Zia Zinka, who could speak perfect Italian. We sent each other many typed letters throughout the years. She was really the heart of the family, keeping in close touch with the family of her brother, my father. Many years later, we corresponded in Italian, exchanging many thoughts. She was the one to organize visits to Fiume, probably bringing Nonna to stay with us a few days. It was difficult to know my cousins because they didn't speak Italian and I could not understand Croatian. I could see their look of futility to our visits, but Zia Zinka was always happy and smiling.

After I came to the USA and learned English, my cousin Nada also learned the language in school. She later came to this country as a visiting professor at UCLA. We were able to get together while she was over here, and when she returned to Croatia, we continued to correspond.

Languages were sometimes a problem in our family. My father's mother could speak Italian and Slovenian, my mother was comfortable only in Hungarian, and in Fiume when I was born, the official language was Italian. Fortunately, my father was fluent in many other languages, except Hungarian. He could not speak to his own mother-in-law, as she knew only Hungarian. In his later years, he had a fairly good mastery of English. Both my parents could speak German, Slovenian, and managed some of the other Slavic languages pretty well, but my father could never learn any Hungarian and my mother was not fluent in Croatian. Italian was the language spoken in our family.

Later in life when I visited Split, I observed a different lifestyle in Zia Zinka's home. The two aunts had everybody sitting at the table while they served us an entire meal. Their custom was to feed the children and guests and they would eat themselves later. In my home in Fiume, we all sat together at meals while my mother would get up only if needed to see that everybody was taken care of.

My cousin Zivko and Nada became very well-educated and even studied until they were well into their thirties. They both played the piano and, of course, the accordion. Nada became a professor of chemistry at the University of Zagreb. She never married, but later made a career in government and became vice consul for Croatia in Trieste (1999). Zivko went into the study of law and eventually became a judge. He married Dessa, an orthopedic doctor. They had two girls, Zlatka and Zinka. Their last name (Rusic) was not passed on, as well as our father's name (Stegel). Brother and sister, the strongest family members, in the end had this shared coincidence. Zia Zinka passed away while her only daughter was here in the USA, on a professorship. Her only son, who was very close to her, tried to call her at home during his working day. That evening, it was discovered Auntie Zinka died quietly alone in her home.

17
Zio Pepi, Uncle

To a five-year-old, Zio Pepi was a wonderful, fascinating uncle, even if I didn't get to see him very often. When, years later, I saw the movie star, Robert Mitchum, I always thought of my uncle. There was a lot of similarity in manners and looks. The relaxed, sometimes distant posture and the slow smile with twinkling eyes was much the same. He was very handsome, and also very loving.

Pepi was my father's younger brother. He was a truck driver and a very good mechanic. Only a few years before, there were only draft horses for transport. The fact that he could drive a big truck made him very interesting to me. No one else among our family or friends could even drive a car. There weren't any cars to drive anyway. However, even in his debonair demeanor, there was something a little sad about this uncle. It became more so in later years. He loved us four children of his brother, I could see it in his expression of joy and fun when he was with us, but we could see him only for short moments now and then. My mother once said, "Emma won't let him come here."

Pepi's wife, Emma, was possessive of her husband. She was not very attractive, with her protruding teeth, but she knew how to dress. She could not have children, so she did not want her husband to be exposed to the happiness of a family. That was what I thought then and think now too. Zio Pepi would sometimes come during his work hours only at the end of the day and would bring a load of leftover fruit, oranges, and apples that were on the verge of spoiling. They were still good for us and they were free.

He was always in a hurry, and my mother said, "He doesn't want his wife to know he is visiting us." In fact, we rarely saw them together visiting us. They had a life as a couple who doted on themselves and never knew the joy and sacrifice of having children of their own. They had a small white Hungarian dog with very long hair that one or the other always had in their arms. Emma always wore a beautiful fur coat as well as lots of jewelry. She was very glamorous. Zio Pepi had a dashing leather jacket, an expensive looking gold wrist watch, and he drove a motorcycle. I always thought people could be jealous of them, including my mother. My parents never had any type of jewelry, not even a wedding ring. I believe they did not think the same way or believed in their style of living. My uncle's life was not involved with families, school, or activities with children. So, as to not displease his wife, he visited us only on these short occasions. He could not permit himself to spend time with our family. A child often sees truth without outside interference. I could see that he loved us, and he loved his wife, too. He was torn between, and he chose his childless wife.

The message I perceived, reinforced by my mother, was that Zio Pepi was not a man to stand on his own. He needed Emma and was easily swayed by circumstances. My mother had issues with this, too, as I remember. They stemmed from her father's experience. Her father, more often than not, had no wages to bring home because he gambled back to the officers the money he was paid by them. He had a weakness for gambling. Zio Pepi had his wife to control him.

My mother's father had been easily swayed by the officers of the Austrian-Hungarian Army to gamble away his tailor's earnings. He made their uniforms, but was easily talked into gambling away what they paid him. My mother equated Zio Pepi with her father's situation. It was hard to understand how somebody could influence another person in this way. My father always regarded comments about his brother with silence. He wished it could be different I am sure.

Life was not happy after the war for Zio Pepi. He and his wife emigrated to New Zealand, with no relatives nearby. He wrote to my father that he was isolated, with no family except his wife. Later, he wrote again, expressing the wish to join us here in the United States. I could see that my father was very sad for his brother. He said, "Zio Pepi is very lonely, and he would like to come here to be with us."

One year, they planned a vacation to Italy and were going to stop here on their way from New Zealand. This never happened. No doubt his wife convinced him otherwise, and they never made it here. His wife really did isolate him from his family. My father became very sad and depressed after this unfulfilled promise.

Years went by and my uncle became ill with throat cancer. His closest friends wrote to us that Zio Pepi spent a lot of time with them in his years there. He talked often about his life in Italy and about our family and other members of his family. They wrote a long letter to us and said he was very lonely. Zio Pepi passed on and his wife remained alone and never made friends. Zio Pepi's friends wrote that she would be well taken care of, as they were well off with properties and other financial savings.

Sometimes, children in one's old age can be disappointing, but not having children at all is very sad. Families are so important, and we don't realize this until it is too late.

18

New Home

After the bombing of our house, and there were several other families also affected, we were without a home. I don't remember where we stayed immediately after that. What I understood from talks was that there were two or three bombs that missed the target and hit the population area. The port below was really the target.

The town authorities immediately relocated us to another part of the city where public housing had just been completed. The street then was *Via Andrea Doria*. Later in life, I was unable to locate this street, as all names are changed as well as buildings. We were lucky to get an apartment on the corner of the first floor of the big concrete building. The apartments were two on each floor, but the next doorway to the building had another row of face to face apartments up to a tenth floor. Across from us, the Dinelli family was moved from another bombed out area. Our families became fast friends and good neighbors. On one side of the building, there were no windows and at the bottom there was a piece of ground with a concrete wall around it, the shape of a triangle. This place was filled with bits of concrete, rocks, and other construction debris. In this small piece of unwanted ground, my parents envisioned the creation of another garden. A potential area for a few vegetables and even a few chickens for eggs.

They quietly started to clear the ground and make space for planting. All the rocks and debris were piled up near the walls that enclosed that area, making another small wall inside the eight-foot concrete wall. The poor soil was turned and enriched with manure and compost collected around the neighborhood. There were still some wagons and horses in use in the city. My mother would really feel good when she could collect a bucket of horse manure. From her youth spent in Hungary, she remembered the horses and the composted farms with fondness.

My father built sheds for rabbits and chickens and, after a while, we had our little bit of paradise in the midst of concrete. It had been therapeutic for them, all the work, and even the change of house. The bombed house had the memories of Sergio and this was a new project.

There were people in the housing development that started to notice and were envious when they discovered this little place of vegetation and life. But we knew they would never had done all the work to create the garden. Instead the area would have just accumulated more and more debris and refuse. All this talk was not important at this point because then there appeared a more serious trouble.

One day I heard heavy steps coming up the stairs to our apartment. I saw two big German soldiers with the swastika on their sleeves. Their boots were very shiny and up to the knee. They had come with a open car and two more were waiting outside. They talked with high-pitched shouts to my mother, as if she was deaf. I was behind her, watching. My mother, who could speak German, was talking to them, but they would not give her much of chance, their voice was much louder and meaner. She appeared so short standing in the doorway, dressed in black as usual, and the Germans appeared to me like giants.

I was trembling behind her, like a little invisible mouse. They did not even see me, I did not make a sound. The SS had arrived and they wanted my brother Ireneo. He was eighteen and they wanted to know his whereabouts.

Their voice indicated questions but I did not understand anything, and my mother was answering in their language. I finally saw them leave in loud noisy steps down to the street. They came back later in four, marching up the few steps from the street.

19

Gypsy Oracle

My mother was a very extraordinary person to me. I used to look deeply in her brown eyes and listen to some of the stories she occasionally would tell me in the happier times of our life.

My mother told me many stories of her life as a young girl in Hungary in 1900. She told me of the sounds of *Czardas* that drew her into the gypsy camp on the outskirts of Budapest. Her family lived within the city close by. The gypsies knew her and she visited them at times during the day when they were cooking, washing, and working around their camp. She looked like a gypsy herself with her dark skin, mahogany eyes and long dark brown hair tied with a red and yellow scarf. Her father's family was unknown, could he have been a child of gypsies?

My mother, Yolanda, knew that gypsies were a common sight around big cities in the Balkan area. Their wagons and horses pasturing in the countryside were part of the scenery in Hungary. The Pustas, a large prairie region, was their adopted home for long periods of time.

Yolanda loved the music of her country, typified by *Czardas* the gypsies played so skillfully on their violins. But this talent was a source of superstition and fear for her friends, for how could simple people with no education play the complicated melodies of the *Czardas*? One girl suggested, "Maybe a devil guides their hands!"

Sometimes, Yolanda was able to sway a friend to accompany her to the gypsy camp. Her friends were fearful and wary of these strange people. They had heard the old wive's tales of their psychic powers. Yolanda was fearless, she loved these people because they were different. She did not believe in superstitions and their music was her soul's expression. One time, Margit, her sister, finally agreed to accompany her. From a short distance, they could see the campfires surrounded with colorfully dressed dark people with their violins. On seeing the girls, gypsies invited them into their circle to sing with them. Their songs were sometimes bursting with life, and then at other times were so very sad, they could bring tears to your eyes. The evening became a crescendo of choruses and captivating music. Margit did not sing. She just listened while studying these expressive people. Her sister Yolanda was caught up in the singing, the gypsies enticing her melodious voice into one song after another.

Seeing Margit so uneasy and reserved, an old woman came up to her and asked, "Do you want me to read your fortune?" Relieved to move away from the noisy campfire. Margit followed the gypsy behind one of the wagons. The old woman looked at Margit's right palm and then the left for a long time with an impenetrable expression on her face. Then she started speaking in a low, clear, whispering voice, "You are in love with a man who will betray you, and you will have a child. This man will leave you and you will suffer. There may be a tragic end that is beyond your control. Take care of your health." Margit shivered. The gypsy went into so many small details about her life that were uncannily true. *Is Andreas going to leave me now that I will have a baby?* she thought. The gypsy watched Margit darkly then disappeared into the shadow of the campsite. Margit returned to stand near her sister.

At evening's end, the tribe accompanied the girls to the edge of the camp and played one last passionate melody of goodbye. The girls chatted on the way home. Margit was uneasy, but more secure with her older sister at her side. "The gypsy read my fortune and told me some things that are true, I am afraid now."

Yolanda replied, "You are just like the rest of them, you believe in nonsense. Our destiny is already planned and life goes on, as it should. You have to live the best way you can." Yolanda tried to quiet her own thoughts as well.

"The gypsy was right in so many things. I now feel a little sick." Margit started coughing and spitting up pink mucous. Yolanda looked closer at her, thinking that Margit was very pale except for her rosy cheeks. She had recently gained unhealthy weight. Disturbed now herself, Yolanda vowed to keep a watchful eye on Margit. She put her arm around her and they reached home safely.

Not many months passed and Margit had a baby girl. Andreas disappeared three months before the baby was born. It was discovered too late that Margit had advanced tuberculosis. She cared for the baby as much as her strength allowed, but before the baby was a year old, she died of consumption. The child was adopted into a farm family.

20
The Stories of the Operas

The opera arias that my mother sang so often had a great meaning for her. I am sure she could associate all the tragedies of the operas to people in her life.

I often would hear my father talking about the irony of one opera or satire of another. My mother often thought about the tragedies. She had experienced some in her real life.

One she often sang was *Butterfly*. This is the story of poor Cio-Cio-San, who waited faithfully for her captain. Her blond blue-eyed son was her whole world to her, in a sad life of waiting. When the father of the boy, an American seaman, comes back to Japan with his American wife, she agrees to give up her child to the couple if Pinkerton himself comes for him. Left alone with her son, her last words, "*Tu piccolo addio*" and, "*Tutto e finito.*" "Little one goodbye, all is finished." Butterfly takes the dagger and reads the inscription. "Die with honor when it is impossible to live with honor." She gives the boy the American flag, sends the child to play, then kills herself behind a screen.

Floria Tosca, a celebrated singer, is a story of political intrigue. The man she loves, Mario Cavaradossi, is an idealist. His rival, Scarpia, is the dreaded chief of the Roman police. Cavaradossi, a painter, is accused of being an accomplice to his friend, Angelotti, who is a political prisoner of the state, having escaped from Saint Angelo castle (a prison in Rome).

Mario, whose political and religious opinions are suspect, is, by accident, involved with the escaped prisoner, Angelotti, who hides in the church where Mario is painting. Mario is taken prisoner accused of political treason. Scarpia, who has his eyes on Tosca, proposes to her a simulated execution for Cavaradossi, in exchange for Tosca herself; she agrees. He signs a safe-conduct for Mario to get out of the country. Tosca, after her final agreement with Scarpia, takes a dagger from the desk as he approaches her and kills him. She then goes to get Mario, but instead finds out he was killed outright. Mario had a regular execution as planned by Scarpia. Tosca discovers the treachery and leaps to her death from the tower of Saint Angelo.

Faust is a sad story. Dr. Faust wants to be young again so he can win the lovely and pure Marguerite. He bargains with Mephistopheles for youth. Marguerite falls in love with Faust and has his child. Valentine, Marguerite's brother, wants to avenge the wrong done to his sister. Swords are drawn and Faust, aided by Mephistopheles, deals Valentine a mortal wound. Marguerite becomes mad with her misfortunes, and kills her child and herself. At the end, her prayer saves her soul, but Faust is taken by Mephistopheles to his kingdom of hell.

Il Trovatore is about the gypsy, Azucena, that, to avenge her mother who was burned at the stake, steals the local count's infant son. She raises him as her own, but one day, the count's other son and the gypsy's son are in a battle, brother against brother. The gypsy's son is killed and the tragedy of her initial actions are uncovered. This was an example of backfire. The son did not belong to her anyway. Retribution sometimes has worse results.

Rigoletto and his daughter, Gilda, who is his whole life, is killed by accident. He had been the court jester and ridiculed all the nobility with his satire and clever jokes.

Then when one of the counts takes his daughter, he becomes the avenger. Sparafucile, who is to deliver the guilty man (the count) to him, dead, instead delivers his daughter, disguised and in a sack. The count was a regular visitor of Sparafucile's sister. The sister, hearing that her brother has the job of killing her count, convinces her brother to save the count (for . . . he brings in money) and just take any man that comes in his path. Rigoletto's daughter comes disguised to their door. Sparafucile probably never even realizes who it really is, but it is the first person that comes in his way, as his sister told him. He just takes her body in a sack to deliver to Rigoletto. Rigoletto laughs, he is now avenged, till he opens the sack.

Turandot, with her three riddles, well disguised in mysterious words. The three words that one must guess are: hope, blood and Turandot (speranza, sangue, Turandot). She is called the princess of ice. Many men have tried to solve the riddles and lost their life. She did not want to be possessed by any man. In order to avenge an ancestor who had been wronged by a man, a suitor had to solve the riddles. The unlucky ones are put to death.

The unknown prince, *il principe ignoto,* wins however. He solves the riddles and this way she becomes his slave. He gives her one more chance to be free. She has to guess his name. At the end, she falls in love with his courage and generous heart. She does not know his name, but he whispers to her that Calef is his name. It does not matter now, because she has decided to love him. We cannot direct our heart, it will direct us.

All the operas have a story that could apply today and the music tells that story. Like the crescendo of the music of *la Forza del Destino.* Life is like a rushing river, and cannot be stopped. It takes along with it all the sad and sometimes happy or funny stories.

All the stories are allegories, or satire, that one cannot take literally, but the hidden meaning is there for understanding human nature.

21

My Mother

She often wanted to talk about her youth. Was it because she wanted to remember that she was young once? She had an interesting life with times of joy, but also sorrow. One time she told me about the *Citta d'Oro* which she visited in Prague. I envisioned a golden city that some day I wished to visit myself. I asked her why it is called *citta d'oro*. She said, "Because in the evening at sunset the city transforms into gold all over." At times, I could see the melancholia in her face when thinking back. I envisioned a city that was all gold, roofs, even streets and I wondered how my mother walked around this city with friends, and happy times. She was in her fifties and I was just twelve or thirteen when I remember her talking about it. I didn't give much importance to it at the time. I was not inclined to listen so much and it seemed so far in history and time, I could not relate then. Later, when I could no longer hear her voice, I had the sorrow that comes from longing to hear my mother talking again. In the recess of my mind, her words filtered back and now I can write them down.

My mother's youth was spent in Hungary (Budapest), where she was born. She remained a true Hungarian, always singing the songs of her country. She taught me how to sing the Hungarian national anthem. It sounded sad, now I have forgotten the words.

She always thought and wished I would inherit her voice, which could have been very similar. Because her singing was so special and sacred to me, I did the opposite. I kept it in my memory and never did sing like she did, maybe because it made me sad.

She told me that her family moved to Fiume (today Rijeka) when she was eighteen. Her father was a tailor and had no family. Her mother (Maria) came from a family of close sisters and brothers (Andreas, Karoly, Sarah and Maria). Maria's two brothers (Karoly and Andreas) and sister immigrated to the United States and made a good life. They attempted to bring the remaining sister, Maria and her family to the U.S. also, but fate did not work for them this way.

My mother told me of the great Hungarian Puszta, a wild and open land, similar to America's Wild West, where cattle herds grazed and outlaws roamed. Here the *csikos,* or cowboys, drove their great herds down from the high steppes before the harsh winter settled in. She had mentioned at times one of the operas she liked *La Fanciulla del West,* or *The Girl of the Golden West,* because she saw the similarity with her country.

Gypsies also roamed these vast grasslands with their hunting music. They cooked goulash over open fires. They roasted ox meat or mutton and whatever they could find or even steal. Today, Puszta is protected by national parks and nature reserves.

My mother told me stories of a certain relative who was a very skilled horseman and a Huszar. She had great regard for this man and talked how well he could handle horses. I didn't realize till years later who this mysterious and exciting man was. It was her uncle Andreas, who was in the prestigious Huszar cavalry. His son, Albert Balogh, explained later in one of our talks about the fact that his father was a Huszar in Hungary before he came to this country. Albert would have been a cousin of my mother.

My mother told me about Sarah, and I remember the name well, but not the details of her life. Sometimes when the conversations would be more interesting to me, I would listen more carefully and it would catch my attention. She talked of a man by the name of Nicholas Kovach in the States who apparently wanted her to emigrate and raise his children after Sarah died. This was the time before my mother was married and she was young. Sarah was my mother's aunt. She also mentioned that of all the children of Maria, mother's mother, my mother was the one that most resembled Sarah, Maria's sister. Many years later in Florida I found out about Sarah's early death from her daughter who was living in the Hungarian elder home. Sarah's husband, Nicholas Kovach, was much older than my mother. No doubt Andreas was involved again in bringing some of his family here by arranging a marriage. My mother was involved in her own life, then married and my oldest brother was born in 1926.

My mother always talked with longing and a sigh about this period of her life when it was probably at a crossroads and life was happening, without being able to control destiny. She must have felt as something had fallen through and she missed out on a new life adventure.

She had a few years of happiness with four children. Later, she shed so many tears for her children. When I was small, I remember the picture she always had on top of the bed, it is almost imprinted in my mind. Now I found it again and when I observe it, I see why she had this picture at the head of their bed. It is a picture of mother and child. The mother is holding the hand of the cherub sleeping among the covers of the bed and tears are falling on her cheeks. Did she see even know then how life would turn out for her and her child? The face of the mother is apprehensive, it is clear she fears for her sleeping child and what life may bring later in life. It was a dear picture then, later it became very sad. It is a symbol of my mother.

22

The Hungarians

The two Balogh brothers, Andreas and Karoly, and their sister, Sarah, were from Budapest, Hungary. They traveled to Fiume at the time when the city was part of the Austro-Hungarian Empire, and Fiume was the third most important port on the Adriatic. From here, they emigrated to the USA sometime around 1893.

In 1902 another sister, Maria, who had married Paolo Soltesz in Hungary, also arrived in Fiume with three children: Margit, Yolanda (my mother) and a son named Paolo named after his father. The family was planning to emigrate at the request of the brothers, who had sent the necessary funds from USA for the voyage. The amount was $500.00, a considerable sum in those days. However, the quota for the Hungarians was filled when the money arrived, so the family was obliged to wait in Fiume until the next quota was opened. Paolo, head of the family, found a good job in his trade as a tailor, working for the army. In the meantime, the money sent by Maria's brothers dwindled away, more children were born, and then World War I started. The dream of emigration vanished.

All the Baloghs had been born in Salamon-Megge, Hungary (before the Soviet rule). Maria, the oldest, was born in 1870. Her husband, Paolo, was born the same year in Kassa (also named Kossice) that later became part of Czechoslovakia.

According to family legend, the Baloghs, Andreas, Karoly, Sarah and Maria, were children of an Hungarian baron and an unnamed courtesan. Their mother was very young and died after the birth of the last child. According to information from Albert Balogh, the son of Andreas, the baron was an irresponsible alcoholic, with an abusing behavior. Maria, the oldest of the four siblings, assumed at a very young age the role of mother and raised the small family.

In his youth, Andreas, became a *huszar* in the elite cavalry of the Austro-Hungarian Army. After coming to the USA, he married Rosa, who was also a Hungarian immigrant. Rosa came to this country alone, with no family of her own, at the age of seventeen. The couple had several children, one of them being Albert Balogh living in Los Altos, California with his wife Ruth.

Sarah also married and has descendants living in Florida. She died at a young age, leaving her husband, Nicholas Kovach, with young children to raise. He later remarried.

Karoly never married and returned to Hungary after a few years and lost contact with the family.

The Soltesz/Balogh family are descendants of the Magyar race and belong to the Reformed Valdensian religion.

Other information as to the origin of Paolo Soltesz is unknown.

The Hungarians have maintained a close community. In older times, they married within their nationality. Today they own and operate an extended-care facility in Palm Bay, Florida, and speak the Hungarian language there. I visited them one year with my Aunt Irene and was amazed that this was a little Hungarian city. The language and food was totally ethnic Hungarian. It brought back memories of my mother's cooking. Here, I met one of Sarah's daughters, who has since passed on. She was in her eighties and could not recollect much about her mother because she was very young when Sarah died.

23

Soltesz Family

One of the pictures I will always remember is of a group of World War I soldiers posed together in an atmosphere of camaraderie. One of the tallest was a blond young man, my father. Close by him is another tall man with dark hair, Paolo Soltesz, my mother's oldest brother.

I heard my father later say how he would often visit this big Hungarian family, so different from his own family. The Soltesz family had several children: the oldest, Paolo (1899– . . .), my mother, Yolanda (1896–1957) Margit (1897–1921), Elena (1909– . . .), Alika (1906–1991), Emilia (1911– . . .), Irene (1913–1994), Arpad (1915–1918).

Margit, of whom I talked about earlier, died of tuberculosis as a young woman. Arpad died as a small child. One story was that he fell on something hard and died not long after an inflammation of the brain, or meningitis. No one was really sure what exactly caused the inflammation or if that was the cause of is death. A fall was mentioned. My dearest Aunt Irene one time said she had been holding the child in her five-year-old lap when he fell. I wondered what was in her heart for years thinking of this incident.

There was another name in the family portrait, Manzi (1903–1917). I am completely in the dark about this young aunt. She died as a young girl. I heard my mother talking about Manzi one time, and she was very sad and distressed. She had tears in her eyes when she said, "What a waste and tragedy." I could feel her heart aching with deep grief.

My mother's mother, Maria, could not speak Italian. To me, she seemed inscrutable, made worse by the fact that she did not say one word in Italian. She was very imposing and good-looking, with salt and pepper hair worn in a large bun on top of her head. I wanted to touch her hair sometimes, it seemed silky, but I did not dare. She seldom smiled, maybe never that I remember. She was not a warm grandmother to us, even after all our attempts to attract her attention. She would shoo us away, then talk at length to my mother in Hungarian . . . she almost appeared angry. We must have irritated her. My mother did not comment on this to us, but my impression was that my mother tried to be soothing to her and pacify her. Maybe telling her, "They are just little girls."

This grandmother lived with her favorite daughter, Elena, of whom she was very protective, and Elena's husband and son. She only had eyes and arms for this grandson, Franco. He was about my age.

I understand now that Grandmother Maria was too old and worn-out to deal with any more children other than the one with whom she lived with. Fate had given her many sad events in her life. Her husband went missing in WWI and she was left alone with many children of a wide range of ages. She was in a country, Italy, where she was a stranger, with a language she could not understand. I had the impression she did not like Italy or anything about it. Three of her children died in very sad circumstances. Even in her own youth, she had the responsibility of her three younger siblings and a father whom his own children never wanted to talk about.

The Soltesz family came to Fiume from Hungary with the intent to immigrate to America in early 1900. Grandmother Maria's two brothers and one sister lived in Chicago and they attempted to have her join them. Maria, however, had many children so this idea was abandoned. Also the funds sent to her by her brothers were used up eventually. The brothers then planned to have the oldest of Maria's children, Paolo, immigrate, but he had to earn a living for the family when the father was found missing in WWI.

The next oldest to be chosen to immigrate was my mother. These uncles of my mother had even a potential marriage for her, a widowed man by the name of Kovac, also Hungarian. He was much older than her and my mother talked about this name with sadness. The name remained in my memory but not much else as I was too young to understand what I'm sure was a complicated story.

All of these plans were happening very slowly with the mail by boat, no telephones, with perhaps weeks or months of ships at sea. The years passed and nothing was accomplished. My mother said once: "It was not my destiny to go to America. It was not meant to be." Mother married my father, Philip Stegel, who she met through her brother Paolo.

The other aunts and uncles on the Soltesz side, my mother's brother and sisters, were all in Fiume and settled here, assimilated in the Italian life. Paolo was *vetraio* or glassmaker, Alika was a barber, Emilia and Elena sent to a *collegio* for a few years, which was just an orphanage where they learned trades such as embroidery. They would always speak among themselves in Hungarian, but their children only spoke Italian and none of us learned Hungarian, as it happens with other languages. I remember only endearing Hungarian words that my mother would speak only to us, such as: dear, sweet children, sweethearts.

We often visited these aunts and uncles, but as it happens today, everyone was very involved with their own family. This was before the war, because afterward we were all displaced.

Aunt Emilia had one son we called Nini. He was much older than my sister and me. Nini (Giovanni) immigrated to Argentina after WWII. He was a civil engineer and I understood he had a very good job there. Later I found out that Nini had died of a sudden heart attack when he was in his forties. Aunt Emilia (Lucchesi, married name) was waiting in Genova to be reunited with him at the time of his death. No one in the family was ever able to get in touch with her. I often thought that she must have died of heartache, as this only son was everything for her, having lost contact with her husband.

Uncle Paolo and his wife, Sophia, had one son. We never really knew this cousin as he was at least twenty years or more older than us. Sophia died young and Zio Paolo remarried later with no children from this marriage. Uncle Alika had two sons, Ezio and Claudio, close to our age, and with whom we still correspond. They live in Northern Italy (Bolzano).

Franco Bogataj was the only son of Aunt Elena. Franco, Ezio, Claudio and our family were pretty close and grew up together. Franco lives in Venice with his family and we also correspond with him often.

Aunt Irene, the youngest of the living children of Maria and Paolo Soltesz, my grandparents, never married. She was at least eighteen years younger than my mother, who raised her for the most part. Aunt Irene was the closest to us children. We were her family and she was our favorite aunt. When she visited us, I used to hear my mother and her talk into late night and together they would laugh as well as cry while they talked about their past. My mother knew a lot about the family, but I believe she only shared the fun times with Aunt Irene most of the time. Later in life,

I would ask about the lost children in her family and Aunt Irene did not seem to know details. I believe she was just too young when all the tragedies happened. One day, she said, "I remember holding a little child in my lap and then he slipped off my lap."

Aunt Irene immigrated to Canada about the same time as my sister and I came to the United States after WWII. She finished high school in Toronto, Canada with a GED and went on to become a nurse. She worked many years in a Toronto hospital and later at Virginia Mason Hospital in Seattle. We were together until her death of heart disease in 1994. She was in her late seventies, but still so very young. I could never think of her old. She gave her heart and life to us and was our second mother. She gave us everything and then was gone from our life, a fleeting dream.

We have distant relatives in Florida and California, descendants of my grandmother's brother Balogh and sister Sarah Kovac. It was Aunt Irene who searched them out. They are her second cousins. No doubt she fulfilled my mother's dream to find her uncle and aunt.

24

Paolo Soltesz, My Grandfather

Paolo, my mother's father, was already long gone when I was born. "Don't mind what anyone felt about your grandfather. Let all that go, and I will tell you the real story," my mother said.

An illegitimate child, he was brought up in an orphanage where he learned the trade of tailoring. There was a hushed story told by my mother's brother and sisters that their father was really the son of a gypsy woman and one of the local landowners. This may be because of his temperament and inclination.

Since Paolo had been placed in a private orphanage, one that taught the children a trade, it followed that he must have been subsidized by some unknown family member. The children that were sent to the poor county orphanages were warehoused at minimum standards, and most certainly were not trained or educated.

In any case, when Paolo became an adult, he had a decent trade which became very valuable. When World War I started, there were many officer's uniforms to be made.

Paolo had one serious character flaw: he was a gambler. He gambled away the money he earned on the very day he was paid. After delivering the uniforms he had made, he was easily tempted into any of the local taverns where he would lose his wages.

He moved to Fiume from Budapest with his growing family, where he became well-known to the officers of the army who were quartered there. Fiume was a bustling port city at that time, of strategic value to the Austro-Hungarian Empire.

Fortunately, Paolo had compensations other than his regular wages. He has sewn a long overcoat for himself with many special pockets inside. These pockets were designed so that many objects could be concealed in different locations. Heavy items, such as sausages, could be easily stored in the upper lining of this coat and the pockets located at the bottom of the coat held such things as bread or candies.

Paolo was a master of sneaking a few items whenever the opportunity arrived. He would come home to the family with a gleam in his eyes and throw his coat open to reveal a wealth of surprises. Gypsies in those days were known for stealing, but Paolo was not considered one and not watched as closely. In my home, we all laughed and loved this story, but it was a family secret.

Later on, during the war, Paolo was drafted into the army. He disappeared and was never heard from again, on the long list of those "missing in action."

My grandmother, Maria, was stranded. She was a Hungarian living in Italy with no extended family. With no income, her family of eight children was difficult to raise. Her two youngest girls, Emilia and Irene, were placed in an orphanage where they grew up speaking Italian. Emilia, older, kept her Hungarian language, but Irene, much younger, could not converse with her mother. Her other children were struggling to make money with various jobs. Paolo, the oldest son, was an apprentice in a glass factory. Alika worked in a barber shop and Elena, more frail than the rest, was talented with embroidery. She could make very precious and beautiful lace work, such as table cloth and many other items that were prized. Yolanda, my mother, worked in a bakery and candy shop.

There were three more children, Margit, Manzi and Arpad, who died during those difficult years.

Maria's two younger brothers and a sister, who had preceded her to Fiume, had emigrated to the USA. Her marriage to Paolo and the many children had doomed her chances to emigrate. Her husband's disappearance robbed her chances for a good life.

Paolo Soltesz and Maria Balogh were both born in 1870. Paolo originated in Kossice, in what is now Slovakia. Maria was raised in Salomon-Magge, near the Carpathian Mountains. The American descendants of her brother, Andreas Balogh, have gone to the area, but were unable to contact any other family descendants of the Balogh. There are no known family members of Paolo Soltesz.

Grandmother Maria lived out her life isolated with only one daughter, because she was never able to speak Italian, and did not seek any other contact other than her family. I was never able to be close to her and she never talked to me. But I had another grandmother that made up for this.

25

A Portrait

The beautiful oval face with penetrating, lively dark eyes in this portrait depicts an animated personality. The date of the photo may have been early 1900s, considering the style of hair, a type of page-boy cut. Her figure was beautifully formed, she could have been an actress.

Aunt Emilia was indeed a fascinating person. She had big brown eyes, dimples, and a smile that was full of life. She was full of energy, and it seemed like she could do almost anything. She had only one child, a boy named Nini, who was much older than my sister and me, he was in college when we were both under four. She was very close to him, and they would go hiking in the mountains, and many excursions on his motorcycle. I often looked at the picture with Nini driving the bike and my aunt sitting sideways behind him, the Alps in the background. No doubt she had bought the bike for him. But even with her job and her son, she still had time to sew many dresses for us!

Carnevale in Italy is a little like Halloween here, but it is celebrated in February, and for most of the month. It is normal to see in the streets of Venice people in costumes going to their jobs and other activities. The *Carnevale* of Venice is very famous for the elaborate costumes, people try to outdo one another. The atmosphere is a happy one at this time. *Carnevale* is celebrated all over Italy, just like Halloween, and children always like to wear all kinds of costumes, but do not go collecting candy.

My mother was not one to participate in fun things

with us. Her life had already known considerable tragedy. Aunt Emilia tried to compensate for her. She came to our house like a whirlwind one day, I remember well, with crepe paper, ribbons, and thread. She cut out petals and leaves from rough crepe paper to make a flower. On my mother's sewing machine, she stitched a beautiful skirt made of round red petals layered to form a poppy, the top black with puffy short sleeves. I actually did look like a poppy with a green hat cupped over my head.

She had another plan for my sister, who was blonde and blue-eyed. She was going to be a bachelor button. The bright blue crepe paper was cut in long thin petals to form a skirt with green leaves as a background: the top was white and simple. This skirt was even more spectacular and there was an elaborate blue layered hat. My sister had become a beautiful flower. I remember that even our faces were painted in a colorful way. Zia Emilia would be sewing on mother's Singer machine with a continuous droning that would stop only shortly now and then. She would take quick measure of our waste, then back on the machine with her hands flying with all the several layers of strong crepe paper. All this was done in a short time and we were ready for *Carnevale.*

Later in life, Zia Emilia did not match what this portrait represented to me then. She raised her son, Nini, to be everything for her, maybe because something was lacking in her marriage. My cousin was a handsome young man, very dashing on his motorcycle, and the pictures of the two stopped at a scenic spot on the road to the mountains, appeared so happy and so perfect. They had fun trips and they were proud of each other. They were happy and it was the best time of their life.

With Zia Emilia's help, Nini was able to graduate as an

engineer from the university. His mother always worked at a good job.

I know that at one time in her life, when Nini was grown, Emilia left her husband, maybe for another man, but nothing came of it and she remained alone. After the war, Nini emigrated to Argentina, where still young, he died suddenly. He was trying to bring his mother to the country. At the time, Zia Emilia was in Genova, waiting to be reunited with him. When this happened, she became completely detached from the family and was not heard from again.

26
Paolo Soltesz (My Uncle)

My mother's oldest brother was Paolo. When their father disappeared in WWI, he had to take over support of the family. Paolo was a good-looking young man with dark skin, black hair and very tall. From the family pictures, I could see his features were very regular. In another picture, I saw him in the military uniform of WWI. So, he also was in the army eventually.

What I remember next is much after that. Zio Paolo worked in a glass factory. It was fascinating to me when I would see him with his magical tool cut a glass for a window.

Paolo had one son with his first wife, Sofia. His name was Puccio, possibly a diminutive for another name. Sofia died when very young and then Zio Paolo married Tina, a much older woman, or at least it appeared to me. They never had any children. Puccio was so much older than I that I can barely remember him, as a very quiet young man. First the illness and then the loss of his mother when just a child must have made a sad imprint.

I was very fond of all the brothers and sisters of my mother and I remember well all their different personalities and uniqueness. Their spouses were not as close to us and I remember Tina especially because I felt she did not like us. Never having children of her own, she was not able to talk to us children and seemed to regard us as strangers.

As it often happens with some men and women, Zio Paolo went along with his wife and did not try to ease up the relationships with the rest of the family. After this marriage, Zio Paolo did not keep in touch with us often and we only saw him occasionally. When we did see him, he always had his wife at his side. He appeared to be holding back his emotions with us, unlike most people, who hug and talk to children. His wife, Tina, was the main person in his life, and even his son was not close to him. Puccio was a growing child when his father married Tina.

Even today, I wonder why we restrict to just one or few relationships rather than love everyone that comes in our life because love is generous and knows no bounds. To remember this is happiness. Happiness is like being at home and home is our heart.

I visited Zio Paolo later in life. After the war he lived in Rome with Tina. We lost touch for many years with the confusion of WWII. Then, one year, with my sons Corey and Chaney, I went to Italy and we met again. He was now happy to see us. They lived in the center of Rome in an apartment. The only son, Puccio, lived in Milano with his wife and son. Zio Paolo could tell me very little about my much older cousin, never having been close to him, and seemed to have little contact.

Paolo and Tina had only each other and together spent most of the time in their apartment while smoking and drinking wine. Paolo worked in a bookstore, but Tina just sat at home and corresponded only with some of her relatives in Yugoslavia. When Paolo died, she went to live there.

27

My Brother, Ireneo/Pippi

My oldest brother was a quiet type, very thoughtful and unassuming. He had been working as a *modelista* in the same shipyard as my father since he was sixteen. Ireneo was his real name used in official papers. His everyday name for us was Pippi. I never knew the origin of this nickname, but it was very dear to me. When I saw a movie with Tom Hanks, I saw Pippi with his blue eyes, the silent gaze that knew so much but was still silent.

I was only about four or five years of age and Pippi was ten years older. He was very tall, at least six feet, blond with blue eyes, extremely soft and tender when he looked at me. I would often sit in his lap and just look at him and feel very secure. I don't remember talking very much and my mother worried about my late start in talking. I heard later that she had taken me to the doctor regarding this. The doctor laughed and said, "Signora, you just wait and she will talk even too much."

When Pippi would come home, he often sat in the kitchen, where my mother was fixing dinner. They would talk and I just looked from one to the other while nestled in his lap. Ireneo had nearly perfect features, nose and eyes perfectly symmetrical. Most of all, I loved his warm, direct gaze. He could look at me for a long time without blinking. Was he thinking he had to keep me well in his memory for the future? His voice was not loud, but that of a young man, soft and clear. He had a very special relationship with my mother. I observed the way they talked, Mother busy with dinner, Pippi talking quietly about his day. I think he was also trying to be of comfort to my mother after the recent loss of my younger brother, Sergio.

My sister, Wilma, two years younger, was busy with small toys on the floor and so Pippi did talk to me a little more. Many times, he would come home with special gifts in his pockets: little doll furniture, table with chairs, cupboard (China cabinet) and sofa with fabric already glued to the seat.

"Look what I brought you. Do you like it?" he asked with joyful, sparkling eyes. He would build small furniture on his lunch hour at work, using little pieces of wood. Pippi was a model-maker in the shipyard. He could design and build anything because this was his special talent and training. He was working at sixteen, right after his training.

Schools are different in Italy. There are five years of elementary education, then three years equivalent to high school here. After the elementary, one could choose to go the route of higher education, which would involve three high schools, *scuole medie,* plus five more years of college. Or a vocational student could choose the trade route with three years of high school, *scuole commerciali.* After that, additional training would be needed as an apprentice in a definite trade. My brother was a qualified *modelista* at age sixteen and working for a small wage.

After the war was underway, I saw a change in Ireneo. He was restless and anxious. After a while longer, gone was his peaceful and patient presence with us. He was not around us like usual. I thought for a while that he was working late and leaving early in the morning.

One day, I was sure he did not come home, and I never saw him again. I missed and longed for his warm hugs, the toys, and the secure and peaceful feeling in the kitchen.

Now I sensed why he always looked so deeply in my face. Did he have a premonition about his life with us?

I finally accepted and knew that he was where he felt he should be. In fact, he had joined the resistance rather than being recruited at age eighteen in the Italian Army. The war years were uncertain. We had been bombed out of our home and had to move. In this new home, I remember my mother receiving a letter from Pippi, not in regular mail, but hand-carried. The orders from Pippi were to read and destroy the letter so as not to incriminate the family.

I heard my mother talking to my father. His letter was sad. Up in the mountains, life was hard, cold, and fatiguing. I saw my mother's tears. She said, "I don't need the letter anymore. The words are sculpted in my heart. They will always be there."

28

Silent Movie

The war was in full force, now the Germans and the Fascists were united. All men eighteen and over had to join the *Camicie Nere*. Pippi had to choose between the fascists or the guerrilla bands in the mountains of the *Venezia Giuglia*, a region that juts out into the Adriatic near Fiume (Rijeka).

My brother Ireneo was just eighteen. His heart had been in turmoil, as I had sensed. It was a hard decision: going into the mountains and leaving his beloved family, or enlisting. The secret that he was gone was kept only a short time. My parents knew he had gone to join the resistance. The Germans were at our door now. I heard the clicking of their boots coming up the few steps to our apartment in the big housing development in *Via Andrea Doria*.

My mother and I were alone in the house. My sister was next door visiting Signora Dinelli, our good neighbor who was always taking Wilma in and gave her cookies and spoiled her. My sister spent entire days there with the Dinellis consisting of a mother, son and daughter, already grown.

The two Germans were huge to me, their heavy steps echoed in the stairs. Their knock on the door was frightening to me. They had a metal helmet and the swastika on their sleeves. They had a pushy presence and were talking very loudly, almost shouting. My mother could speak German and was answering questions and talking to them. As I hid behind her, I heard the soldiers rough voices becoming louder and more intimidating. My father was at work and could not protect us.

I was watching all of this scene like a silent movie, I could not understand anything and was fearfully hiding behind my mother. They were not going away and then finally my mother, without explaining, sent me over to the Dinellis. She said, "I have to go with them, and you stay here with your sister until I come back." She did not explain any further, and I could see she was very anxious.

Mother was taken to the headquarters. She was actually arrested and taken to the station between the two soldiers, like a prisoner. Nobody was notified and when my father came home from work he learned from the neighbors what happened. He went immediately to the headquarters where my mother was held and negotiated an exchange.

Now I knew that my brother was a partisan and this was the reason for the Germans in our life. He had not enlisted in the army and Germans were unforgiving. They could even find a Jew as a needle in a hay stack, but a traitor or rebel was even worse to them.

My mother came home the next day, but not my father. I am sure they had to go through much investigation and final agreement to let Mother go home. This was an exchange and he was held hostage for my brother. My mother and I went to the prison many times for visits, but nothing was accomplished. The process of interrogation was a military routine that took a few weeks, then without notification or warning to our family, my father was sent to Germany. He spent the rest of the war at hard labor in a political concentration camp. This was not a death camp: there was no gas chamber or oven, but the prisoners lived in unheated barracks surrounded by barbed wires and very little food.

There were many concentration camps in Germany. They were all dehumanizing. I don't remember the name of the camp where my father was sent, though I would recognize it if mentioned.

The Germans must have had some intelligence that knew my brother was a partisan. I know of one instance where a mother hid her son underground out in the country and he was saved as well as his family. My parents' statements that they did not know where their son was did not help. They drilled them and shouted at them that they knew where he was.

One last time, we went to the headquarters to find that father was not there anymore. Mother demanded information as to what happened to him. The German officers there were scornful and even amused by my mother. Their policy was always to withhold any information about prisoners. One of the officers was a tall, blond man with handsome features, but a cruel smile. He told her, "We don't know where your husband is!" He talked in Italian in a thick accent, even though my mother could speak German to them.

We left with my mother leaning on me, tears running down her face.

29
Borsa Nera (Black Market)

Mother was very sad. Now there were only three of us left of a family of six. The fate of my father was uncertain, as well as my brother. Did she foresee a future of more losses? I kept observing quietly as my mother was mostly silent. I was also very quiet, talking minimally, unlike most girls chattering away. May have been that she had too much grief to share and burden a child. At this time nearing the end of the war, I was nine.

Our neighbor Signora Dinelli finally came to her rescue, and gave her a good talk about her duty of having to take care of two daughters. Talks were never shared with us children, but sometimes I was able to sneak around and hear. I kept everything to myself and never asked questions, maybe because I felt helpless and was not encouraged to talk.

After a while, Mother gathered some courage and her spirit seemed to lift a little, especially since Dinelli gave her a job. The job was to take tobacco and other goods to exchange with farmers for potatoes and other vegetables. She had to find out what was needed and what could be exchanged. This involved a lot of bartering. Dinelli had a little store in her house.

During this time, Mother risked her life with all the trains being blown up. She had to go to the farms in outlaying villages, the only transportation was the train and walking. When I understood what she was doing, I would not physically let her go without me. Even Dinelli could not tear me away and I would cry really loud and run after her when I got loose from the grip of our neighbor.

A few times, I just went like that, tagging along, then I was outfitted with a smaller back pack and this pack was also full of goods and heavy. We would leave together early in the morning.

We would come back late at night, alone in the dark streets, loaded with packs of food. Dinelli was always ready to take everything that same night, and Mother would take home food to feed us with. There was no income at all coming in, and the apartment was public housing, probably very low rent. No such thing as public assistance, as there is today when nobody can earn a wage in a family.

This is how we survived during the war.

Like my dear Slovenian grandmother said, *"Manje ali slaste"* less but sweeter, and we felt lucky.

Father's family; children: Pepi, Zinka, Filippo, Milka

My father

Our family: Leda, Ireneo, Father, Mother, Wilma, Sergio

Ireneo, Sergio, Leda, Wilma

Brothers Pippi (Ireneo) and Sergio

Our magical garden in Fiume

Our family without Sergio

Wilma and Leda

Brother Sergio, 1940

Our neighborhood before the war

**Ireneo
(1926–1944)**

Balogh-Soltesz family: Irene, Ali (Alfredo), Emilia, Mother Maria

Margit Soltesz (Maria Balogh's first daughter)

My mother, 26 years old, 1923

Fiume 23 X 1930

Mia Carissima Zia Zinca;

Con immenso dolore ti annunciamo la morte del nostro Caro Sergio. Che è avvenuta il 25 di settembre alle 10 di sera.
La mamma e papà sono tanto addolorati che non possono scriver neanche alla nonna perchè hanno paura che le farà male. Per questo ti scrivo a te; il 16 settembre il giorno fatale, Sergio e cascato da un'albero di fico, ha fatto una ferita sotto il ginocchio; papà lo ha portato subito all'ospedale dove gli hanno fatto tre punti, otto giorni stava bene, ed in una volta il male si aggravò e subentrò il tetano, venne portato con l'autobulanza all'ospedale di nuovo dove, dopo due giorni e due

Letter from Boris, October 23, 1930

notti con atroci sofferenze moriva.
Gli 22 furono fatto il funerale che riuscì
assai bello.
Intervennero molti bambini e ragazzi
suoi amici colle famiglie, il coro dei ragazzi che hanno cantato il Miserere,
e molti conoscenti fra i quali anche la
signora Rode e tanti vostri conoscenti.
La nonna Soltess tanto piange e non
si può consolare, e giusto ieri è andata
ad abitare da zio Paulo perchè qui tutto
le ricorda Sergio che gli voleva tanto bene.
Io Ti ho scritto tutto quello che sapevo
un giorno si deciderà forse anche papà e
scriverà meglio alla Nonna.
Sergio un angioletto che pregarà per noi tutti;
qui Ti aggiungo una coppia del culto che
il nostro Pastore ha tenuto al cimitero
saluto in nome di tutti noi Voi tutti.
       Boris

LA VO

IZI

L'ultimo saluto ai compagni Zorzenon, Poscani e Stegel

In un'atmosfera di commossa raccoglimento si sono svolti ieri nel nostro camposanto i funerali solenni dei compagni Stegel, Zorzenon e Poscani.

Oltre alle rappresentanze civili e militari erano presenti centinaia di concittadini che hanno voluto portare l'ultimo saluto alle tre giovani vittime della barbarie nemica.

I lavoratori dei Cantieri Navali compagni di lavoro dei caduti, Zorzenon e Stegel, hanno assistito numerosi alle onoranze funebri ed un gruppo di essi, diretti [...] Venuto, hanno cantato con ispirato sentimento «La preghiera dei trapassati» suscitando la commozione dei presenti. Particolare significativo è il fatto che il coro dei Cantieri ha cantato ieri per la prima volta dopo 20 anni di forzata inattività.

L'ing. Deluca e l'operaio D'Arsilio hanno tenuto due brevi discorsi ricordando il sacrificio degli scomparsi e rinnovando nelle loro tombe la promessa di continuare sulla via tracciata da quelle idee di rinnovamento sociale, in nome della quale essi hanno dato il loro giovane sangue generoso.

Poscani, Zorzenon e Stegel, compagni di fede e di lotta rimarranno sempre nel ricordo e nella riconoscenza del nostro popolo.

Eroi del popolo

Fiume - 1946

Era il tempo ardente della lotta di liberazione. I giovani capaci di dire no al servaggio, erano partiti e diventati partigiani, sfidando la potenza dell'oppressore. Tra essi Ireneo Stegel [...] e Zorzenon Germano: il primo diciassettenne, inesperto dell'arte militare, il secondo ventiseienne, veterano di sei anni di marina, ma animati tutti e due dall'entusiasmo per una vera libertà e giustizia sociale Ed essi furono fedeli all'ideale ed alla consegna fino all'ultimo. L'alba del 7 agosto 1944 segnò la fine del loro combattimento.

Laggiù, sulle ridenti colline dell'Istria, con 15 compagni, si erano appostati fin dall'alba in una pineta prospiciente la strada provinciale, nell'attesa del nemico. Vennero i tedeschi ed i fascisti, bene armati, montati su diversi autocarri, diretti ad un rastrellamento. L'attacco fu immediato ed efficace, ma, avutasi ella superiorità numerica, i partigiani dovettero ripiegare. Ireneo e Germano furono incaricati di proteggere con la loro mitragliatrice la ritirata dei compagni. E là caddero, compiendo il dovere di soldati del popolo fino all'ultima cartuccia.

Oggi, a due anni di distanza, li ricordano i compagni, li piangono i genitori, che tanto li amarono e vissero lunghi mesi in carcere e in campo di concentramento, nell'incertezza della loro sorte. E gli amici tutti portano sulle loro tombe il fiore della riconoscenza.

Ricordiamo, compagni Steghel e Zorzenon il vostro sguardo sereno e dolce, la fiducia sempre nascente nei vostri cuori, la vostra bontà d'animo pronta al sacrificio. Fedeli ed umili eroi, ci ammoniate col vostro esempio che la vita umana acquista il suo vero senso e la sua vera forza soltanto nel seguire fino alla fine la via e l'ideale, che la nostra coscienza c'impone e che il nostro cuore ardentemente desidera.

Crisantemi sui marmi

Giorno dei morti.

I più tristi ricordi incidono oggi nell'anima un profondo solco di dolore, un lutto lontano nel passato raffiora e involge di malinconia ed alla pesante meditazione sulla caducità umana, un lutto recente esacerbisce la disperazione e fa più amare le lacrime.

La pia tradizione vuole che questo giorno sia consacrato in onore dei nostri morti, di tutti i morti.

Sulle salite che portano al Camposanto cittadino, centinaia, migliaia di persone portano ai loro cari scomparsi il saluto di una preghiera e l'omaggio gentile dei simbolici fiori, che nulla serra nuda, sulle croci di legno, sulle pietre e sui marmi s'orna di policromi e rabbrividisce con lo tepore calda bellezza la gelida rigidità dei sepolcri.

Tutti i morti! Quanti, dopo questa immane guerra si piangono, e non tutti riposano li sotto i cipressi di Cosala, in seno a quella stessa terra che ne ha sentito le vite! Madri, spose e figli sono stati preceduti dall'orrenda ferocia di questo apocalittico conflitto anche dal conforto di piangere sulla tomba, per umile del loro Caduto; ed il loro dolore piagnificasi ogni, come una fiume in piena senza sbocco.

Tutti i morti! — E l'odio per chi ha causato tante rovine nella materia e negli spiriti, s'attenua — in questo giorno sacro — nella coscienza del dolore universale, che un'uguale sofferenza come una tremenda piaga, tormenta il mondo intero; e si posa anche sulla squallida tomba senza rifiuto di un ignoto nemico un fiore generoso come un pensiero di carità e di perdono.

Papaso, curvi, donne brunate, uomini a passi gravi, i bimbi timidi e silenziosi tra i culti del cimitero, si sembrano immersi in un alone di mistico raccoglimento, sopra i tremuli lumini, i calici mesti dei pini averni, i boschi e le mortelle. Lento e sommesso s'ode il brusio delle orazioni e l'aria tutta s'impregna dell'acuto profumo di mille crisantemi e di mille fiori.

Ma non è solo fra i marmi tombali del Camposanto che s'eleva un pensiero memore e accorato in onore di chi non è più; in ogni casa ed in ogni famiglia è celebra e si sente la religiosa solennità di questa giornata.

Oggi, ogni ricordo è una preghiera.

Uncle Paolo, Fiume, 1934

Irene, 1939

Aunt Milka, Nonna Stegel, Nada, Zivko

Terrace, Villa Vittoria

Sun room, Villa Vittoria, Leda, 1950

Father and mother, 1950

Nada, Zivko, Zinka, Milka, 1955

30

A Life of Perils

In the housing development where we moved after the bombing, we were next door to the Dinellis and my mother became close friends with Signora Dinelli. This interesting woman was a wheeler-dealer in many ways. She had a mini-store in her apartment where she would buy, sell, or trade anything of value. She made enough money to take care of her family: a son and a daughter both in their late teens. The son Ranato was unable to work because of a debilitating bone disease, so he was studying for a college degree in design or architecture. He had to walk mostly with crutches, sometimes with a cane, when he was feeling better. He was also a dedicated sculptor and we still have some of his marble art. Lea, the daughter, had an office job and her earning helped her mother. The three were very close, and in this instance, I could really see that "blood is thicker." Lea had a fiancé, but after many struggles between them I heard they separated because Lea would not leave her mother and brother.

Sometimes I watched with fascination as Signora Dinelli weighed sugar, flour, or potatoes on her big steel scale. She measured with much precision, but then would throw in an extra potato or add a little more sugar.

My mother was one of the people who brought goods to sell. I knew my mother risked a great deal in this venture but this was all she could do when my father was gone and she had to provide for her two remaining children. The

Borsa Nera was a way of life and a means of survival for many other people besides us.

In the struggle between the occupying German army and the Italian guerrilla bands, there were many trains blown up, especially at night. These were the little local trains that my mother had to take to get out of town to the farms where she bartered with farmers. In her backpack, she would carry clothes, blankets, cigarette and other things that the farmers needed. She would come back with much heavier loads, backpacks filled with potatoes, corn flour, turnips and many other goods. She was a very good trader.

When she would leave, my sister and I were the charges of Signora Dinelli. Eventually I realized what my mother was doing and I insisted on going with her. Nothing would stop me, not even repeated spankings.

Now and then I heard people say, "Another train blew up last night!" My mother was aware of the danger, but she had no other choice. She had faith that we would be lucky. We had to survive, and there was no other income. Sometimes, the two of us had real fights, but I would not let her go alone. She tried to sneak off sometimes, but I would wake up, grab my bag, and run after her. Our trains never blew up during the day although those same trains were sometimes derailed during the night.

Mother had also another job: the Jews.

31

The Psychic

When we moved to our new home in town, my sister was about five or six and I was two years older. Signora Dinelli was across the hall from us in an apartment building where two units faced each other, and two more up to last floor, which may have been six floors. She became very close to my mother right away, as if they had been old friends. I never knew her first name, as children we never called any older person by first name. It would always be: *Signor* or *signora, signorina* if not married.

Dinelli was a widow and brought up her children, Lea and Ranato, all alone, usually a rare happening. Most families in Italy have many relatives around them. This family had only themselves. There was an older son, but he was living in New Zealand. Lea, a very athletic and a good-looking blonde, was engaged a long time, but at the end, it did not work out and her fiancé left her. Renato, also a striking young man, never planned to be married because of his condition, which they called tuberculosis of the bones. He was always very busy with studying, drawing, or sculptures. He later became an engineer and worked in a big company near Torino.

Besides trading goods, Signora Dinelli also read the tarot cards, but only on special occasions and only for certain people. She was a true psychic. She could anticipate my thoughts without me saying anything. Everything in her house was so interesting and busy. People were coming and going, bartering and selling goods that one could not find at the regular store, or too expensive. Dinelli was able to sell things like cigarettes cheaper, and some things were just not available except in her store.

This was all part of the black market, or *contrabando* as we called it. It was somewhat secretive in a way, maybe only from the regime.

Tarot card reading was also a good source of income, but she would *butta carte* only to people she felt so inclined and during these times we were not allowed in her house. Children were not to be present during her card reading, it was one of her rules. Signora Dinelli even looked like a witch, only a good witch, as she often took care of us. She limped with one leg, much shorter than the other. She had green-gray penetrating eyes, but benevolent. The blondish white hair was in a bun but the fine hair was flying all over anyway. Her nose was short and turned up with wide nostrils from frequent use of snuff. She was blowing her nose often after the snuff, followed by much sneezing. She always had her big white hankie in her pocket. It seemed to me that she snuffled every time I looked at her. She was meticulous in her habit and her dresses were always very clean. She wore an apron that covered most of the dress. She would brush off any snuff that got on her clothes.

Once she read the cards to my mother, probably at her insistence. Later, I heard my mother talking to a friend about it. Dinelli was reluctant to read cards, especially to my mother, who may have had some unhappy omens, but she tried always to tell only the good things.

"She told me she saw me up on a hillside walking slowly, the hill was a grape orchard. She said I was picking the white grapes, but these represented tears." I heard her say to another housewife.

Mother talked about other details of the reading, and I

know it disturbed her. She had insisted herself on the reading. I knew Signora Dinelli was remarkably good with those cards. I had heard other people talking about it with amazement. She was also very careful in not saying bad things, but people always read more into it.

Signora Dinelli took care of us very often when my mother started on the bartering and traveling to the farms. She was probably the one person that saved my mother in the hour of a severe distressed mental status. During this time, there were no aunts and uncles visiting. We were all alone in a new home and everybody just struggled alone. Nobody associated with partisan families openly or they would be killed by the Germans. My Uncle Ali also was sent to a concentration camp I later found out.

32

The Jews

There were many Jewish people in Fiume who were being rounded up by the Germans. They were then held prisoners in buildings in an area between Fiume and Susak.

My mother had taken on another job. She was entrusted by relatives of these victims that still had their freedom to take food and special items from home to their loved ones. Usually food and some clothes.

Fiume was not a huge city and word of mouth would travel well. My mother knew some Jewish people. She was known for being kind and fearless. The poor Jewish people who had relatives taken in the camps asked her to take these items to their dear relatives held there.

I remember going with my mother on these trips, with baskets of food, sandwiches, and cookies lovingly put together to send with her to their relatives. We both would carry a basket carefully, as not to disturb anything that it contained. She almost acted as if we were carrying gold.

Unfortunately, these were only halfway destinations. From here, people were shipped by train to concentration camps.

Walking alongside Mother, we presented ourselves to the guards of the building. She spoke in German, asking them to deliver the baskets to the family members held there. They had the family name on the bundles. The baskets were taken and hopefully delivered. We never saw the inside of the prison. The huge gate was closed and the guards were posted outside.

One time or maybe two, the guards would turn us away, baskets and all. I only sensed that the people had already left for Germany, and were no longer there. I could not understand anything they said in German and my mother seemed unable to explain to me. She must have been too emotionally upset to articulate the fact that these prisoners had been sent to the death camps in Germany or Poland.

However, my immediate and first thought was that now we had to walk back to Fiume with the baskets full of food. I was usually very hungry. After a lot of talking to the German guards my mother would turn back silently and my chin would drop on my chest as we slowly walked away. After a little while, I asked mother if we could look in the basket and see if there was something to eat.

She would open finally one of the bundles and gave me some cheese and salami sandwich. I can still taste it, it was so good. Mother would not eat anything, she just walked silently and looked very sad. She would not have the heart to tell the relatives that the baskets had not been delivered because their families had already been shipped to the camps.

This is how she was able to decide to give me the food in the basket. She usually would take me home and I never saw her confronting the families on our return. Walking beside her, I could feel what was going through her mind and I understood when I saw the tears.

The relatives of the Jewish prisoners had entrusted their precious food from home for her to take to the prisons because they could not take it. They would be arrested themselves if they went to their brother, father, or son with goods from home. They trusted my mother with this task. She was not afraid to risk her life for these poor people, suffering in the holding camps or still at a mercy of only time.

The Germans were systematically arresting all the Jewish people. There also were death on people aiding either the Jew or the partisans. These people were regularly executed. Mother was an ally and a friend of the Jews. Farmers in the outlying villages were also executed for hiding or aiding the partisans, even if they were only suspect.

My mother must have been pretty good at talking to the guards in German, and they were not really treating her badly. I remember they were just young grown kids. They may have seen her as a mother. She was happy when they would take the bundles and promise to deliver them.

The Jewish people were grateful to her. They slipped some money in her pockets, for she did not want anything. She said they all would cry with her about their predicament and they would console each other.

The Jewish people suffered as well as other people who had to witness the cruelty of an insane war led by insane people.

33
Silence at Susak Bridge

An excitement was in the air. I could hear voices all around me, in one side or the other of the big apartment complex and in the street. The excited tone of voice of people echoing here and there. As I went outside the house, I could hear distant cries. Children were running excitedly toward downtown, crying out, *"La guerra é finita."* I stood still, just listening as the voices faded in the distance.

Downtown was not very far from where we lived in our second home, just a few blocks, but I also ran there after I realized the festive atmosphere. I wanted to see the excitement, but Mother was quiet in the kitchen and not moving. My sister with the Dinellis and not moving either.

The allies were pouring in the main street of Fiume in their jeeps, tossing candy and gum and wrapped chocolates. All the children scrambled while the adults crowded close to the jeeps and trucks, trying to hug the soldiers as they were going by. It was so exciting and I was full of joy. I came back home to tell what was happening in the streets. My mother was quiet.

The excitement lasted a few days as people were mingling with the GIs in the town, watching them as if they were from another planet, and they poured love on them. We loved the debonair look, their smiles, their energy, their easy-going way. As a child of nine, I watched them with awe.

My mother was not involved in all of the celebrations, even when she did go downtown with me to see the allies, she was only watching silently far from the crowd. She was apprehensive. My father was still in some unknown place in Germany and my brother was in the mountains with the partisans.

My sister was usually in the care of Signora Dinelli, so it was mother and I that one morning started to walk in the streets that led to Susak Bridge, the border between Italy and Yugoslavia. I remember when we arrived at the square in front of the bridge and the details of the scene there. The typical *piazza* where several streets entered from the city was full of people. On each side of the bridge, there was a cyclone fence, but the gates of the bridge were wide open. The river separated the two towns, Fiume and Susak.

Over this bridge, groups of partisans, ragged and dirty, were coming through either in groups or in twos or threes or alone. They were members of the *Stella Rossa*, a brigade of partisans from that region. As they crossed the bridge and came into the piazza, they would increase their pace, then run to some waiting relative. The piazza was filled with small crowds and everyone was looking anxiously at the bridge. The fortunate reunited would walk away happily.

Mother and I were standing a little ways from the bridge, under the shadow of a huge tree. It seemed to me as if we were almost hiding and didn't belong to that crowd. Mother was quiet, her hand on my right shoulder. I was just nine and many times she had told me how I was just right height for her to lean on. I was her faithful cane. Mother had been injured as a little girl and almost lost her leg. She had been caught under the wheel of a wagon after a team of horses spooked while she was walking to school. Her knee had been fused in place after this accident.

In the corner of the piazza, the two of us were waiting. I had a strange feeling of isolation and sadness, but I was silent. So separated from the rest of the people there, Mother was only watching the bridge. We stayed there most of the day.

Deep down, I knew that our waiting was futile. There had been some rumors for some time that my brother had been involved in confrontation with the Germans. Nothing official, and it was not discussed with family or friends.

The number of partisans coming home was dwindling, and finally, at eveningtime, only a very few were coming through. They all looked very tired. They had walked a long ways from the mountains. They all had suffered cold and hunger while on continuous alert. Now, Mother had courage to go to one of them asking, "Did you see my son . . . a tall blond boy, *un giovane biondo.* His name is Ireneo?"

"*No, Signora, mi dispiace.*" He'd shake his head, as did the others that followed. Most of the partisans knew each other, but they acted as if they didn't know. Maybe they did not have the heart to tell my mother the fate of my brother.

I felt an emptiness inside me and an indescribable ache all through my body. I looked up at my mother and saw tears. She quickly wiped them off with the back of her hand. I said, "Mama!" and put my arms around her. I couldn't help but cry. She didn't say anything, her throat was closed up, but her eyes told me not to say anything now. We hugged together, I cried so much. We were alone, had nobody but each other and there was nothing I could do because my pain for her was even greater than my own.

At the end of the day when it was getting dark, the *piazza* was empty, everybody had gone home. Mother and I, all by ourselves, finally turned to go home. We walked slowly, looking back a few times, but the bridge was empty. With my head down on the pavement, Mother leaning on my shoulder more firmly, more for comfort than support, I was trying very hard to hold back my tears. I was her only comfort now, I had to be strong. The premonition that her son was not coming home made me more aware that she needed my shoulder for warmth and assurance and the reason that she had me with her. I was glad now that I would not have let her go without me anyway.

Signora Dinelli, the psychic, had tried to interpret Mother's earlier dream gently. The white grapes in the mountains. She was known for her accuracy of future events told by the Tarot cards. Now, it came back to me.

The war was over, but it didn't matter now. It was not important.

34

Partisans

The German Army was relentless in attacking small towns and the countryside where they suspected partisan activities. The partisans shifted their locations in the mountain areas all over Italy. They were always moving from one area to another and the people of the area were always helping them. The Germans were regularly making raids in these villages. Sometimes, they would line up a group of people against a wall and just execute them, only because they were suspected of harboring a partisan. It was true that the people were allies of the partisans. Some were neutral but sooner or later, they would assist in one way or another. There were very few men in these villages, and most of them were older men. All their young men had already gone to the army, either Italian or with the partisans. I know of one instance, however, where a mother managed to hide her son underground all during the war; this way he escaped either side of the fighting. Her son escaped the danger of war but many more did not. Jack Olsen, North-West writer, who was in the Special Forces, documented the war in the book *Silence at Monte Sole.* This book relates what happened in the area near Bologna, which was attacked seriously by the Germans. Other areas in the mountains were also attacked continuously in their task to wipe out the partisans.

In Istria and Venezia Giuglia, where my brother was fighting, there were large groups of partisans under the name of *Stella Rossa*. These brave groups were hiding in the mountains and caves of the area. They had a hospital set up in the woods. They used areas where there was a river to evade the Germans and their shepherd dogs. Partisans would carry their wounded across the river on their shoulders, a long way into the mountain hospital. The dogs could not follow the scent and the Germans would turn around and retreat. There were also many partisan women, one became well-known because she was also a doctor and came to help with the wounded.

Today, there are landmarks and memorials in these areas. I believed the forest hospital is also preserved. This is to remember how much hardship these guerrilla bands had. They had scarce ammunitions while the Germans had many different types, including truck carrying loads of soldiers armed with grenades, machine pistols, and machine guns. I would see soldiers around town always with belts and grenades and their machine pistols which they used to execute. I can still remember the sound of rapid fire of their guns. The casualties of the partisans were great, but they had the villager support in the same manner that the concentration camps prisoners had the sympathy of the farmers around the camps. There are memorials of this war everywhere.

35
Ireneo

Eventually, after the war, my mother learned how my brother had been killed in the hills of Istria.

After placing us in secure lodging (orphanages) arranged by our pastor, she went on her quest to find out what happened to my brother. This was before my father even came back from Germany.

She went to the farmers of the area around Buie, and they were able to report all the details they watched from their bolted homes. They had word that the Germans were about to make a *rastrellamento* and they locked themselves in their homes. From the windows, they saw the Germans advancing with *carri armati* working their way up the mountain village. The partisans were all over the area. The Germans were numerous and aggressive.

My brother and another boy were assigned on the promontory to defend the retreat of the partisans group. They were to keep the advancing Germans at bay while the larger group of partisans were escaping. The plan then was that before the Germans were upon them, they would also escape.

The Germans advanced quickly with heavy gunfire, a third partisan was also killed during this retreat. My brother and his comrade remained on the hill with two machine guns and limited ammunition. Suddenly, when their last cartridge was used up, the Germans were upon them. From below the little hill, they held them down with their guns. Their carri armati (tanks) had big enough guns to blow the whole hiding place.

The two boys held their arms up to surrender. The Germans discussed a few minutes among them, but the leader gave the final order to shoot, saying, "These are the real traitors."

The farmers who witnessed did not spare any details: the two boys were machine-gunned down across their chest. Two brave members of the *Stella Rossa* were dead. The priest of that village and the villagers buried the two youth in their cemetary.

My mother in her grief could not console herself. She went back to Fiume and secured a truck. She returned to Buie and had the two disinterred and carried their remains in the back of the truck to Fiume. She was sitting between the two coffins during the two-hour trip back to Fiume. Here, she had a funeral that was reported in the papers. Now the two are also buried in the cemetary in Fiume reserved for the partisans and the members of the resistance. Others in their group are buried together in the same area among the vast number of partisan graves.

36

The Funeral

A proper funeral was arranged with our pastor for both youths that died together. My mother was not going to let them die unknown, for the "cause." All the relatives and friends of the two boys were walking behind the two caskets and many more people created a procession of sorrowful people. They walked with heavy pace among the dark avenue of the cemetery. They were immersed in their thoughts in a quiet procession under the weeping willows, the pines, and boxwood that lined the avenues.

Subdued whispers of prayer could be heard and the air was impregnated with perfume of thousand of chrysanthemums and other flowers. In the cemetary, among the marble stones, the people remembered with honor those who passed on.

In Italian cemetaries, all graves have a fixed time period with expiration date. Then the remains are removed to a mausoleum or communal grave. The grave space is then used for another departed for a period of years. However, the graves of the partisans will be left untouched and preserved for generations. Their marble stones with the red star are among hundreds of those who fell for their ideals of a better society.

The funeral of my brother and the other youths, Germano Zorzenon and Poscagni, was covered in the local newspaper under the headline, HEROES OF THE PEOPLE.

37

Camps

There were many concentration camps. The worst were the "death camps," for Jews only—Auschwitz, Dauchau, Trablinka, Birkenau. There were also "work camps," where political prisoners were made to do terrible jobs—such as clearing the bodies of the gas chambers. If they refused, they were executed themselves.

My Uncle Alika was a barber by trade. His shop in Fiume had been a gathering place for men who wanted to talk about politics and speak against the regime. These discussions were done in secret, but soon or later, the Germans came to know about them. My uncle became a political prisoner. He was interned in a camp in Germany, where his job was to shave heads. The Germans did everything in their power to separate families, so my father, my uncle, and all of their friends were systematically assigned to different camps. They didn't learn of each other's fate until after the war.

When the war was over and the camps were liberated, my father, now looking like a skeleton, was lucky to have escaped death from starvation or disease. There was a lot of dysentery, and many people died in the political camps.

All the prisoners started to walk out of the camps. My father started his walk from Germany to Italy. Many times during this time, he was able to get rides from allied soldiers passing by. When he finally came home to Fiume he was in rags, unshaven, skin and bones.

I was not home at this time. My mother with the uncertain fate of my father and my brother having died a partisan in combat, had arranged for us to stay at an orphanage. Later, I saw pictures taken for purposes of an identity card, when it didn't look like my father at all, but rather like a derelict.

Mother could not really take care of us two girls when she was in a desperate state of mind, waiting to hear if our father was alive, and knowing my brother gone. In fact, the minister may have arranged for someone to be with her. Her state of mind was such that she wanted to die, I am sure such was her grief after losing her first two children.

My father seldom spoke of his experience in the camp. I heard fragments of conversations later. He talked about the farmers that raised potatoes in the fields outside the camp. These people were kind and generous to the prisoners, and helped them survive. These camps were not as strictly supervised, so the prisoners could slip through the wire at night and glean potatoes from the fields. The farmers knew this and let them take anything. The prisoners would cook the potatoes on open fires and they survived this way.

I heard my father say, "German people were good. It was their government and military that were destructive." In fact, I never heard my father speak with any hint of prejudice toward any kind of people. All I remember is the equality he so desired for all men. He often said how it was necessary that all people have equal benefits and equal rights for life.

38

The Revenge of the Partisans

On the evening of April 25, 1945, Benito Mussolini and Claretta Petacci were fleeing from Milano trying to escape into Switzerland. They attempted to reach *La Valtellina*, a region near the borders of Piemonte and Lombardia. The partisans caught up with them on the 27th at Dongo near Lago di Como and placed them in a farmer's house overnight in Bonzanigo.

Almost all the farmers were allies of the partisans, always helping them either to hide to give them food, or report information of the German strategy. Many villages, however, were discovered helping the partisans and many people were executed by the Germans. People helped at risk of their life.

On April 28th, Colonel Valerio of the *resistenza* arrived from Milano with Aldo Lampredi, called Guido. During the war, Valerio was a pseudonym of Walter Audisio. Walter is not an uncommon name in northern Italy, being exposed to other countries which are more liberal in names, while south Italy remain traditional, naming children after saints. The two were well-known leaders of the partisans of the group of *Stella Rossa*. Another leader in the region of Emilia was called *Lupo*, also a well-known partisan. The two leaders had several partisans with them, members of the band. All the different bands were bitter adversaries of the Nazis.

Benito Mussolini and La Petacci, his lover, were taken by automobile to the nearby village of Giulino di Mezzegra.

Here, in front of the gate to the estate of Villa Belmonte, they were shot. Valerio, the executioner, had trouble with his machine pistol, which jammed. This was a gun manufactured by the Germans, light, small, and usually effective, which had been captured in quantity by the partisans. Another of the partisans band handed his own machine pistol to Valerio as a replacement.

According to legend and witnesses, Claretta was not in the plan for execution, but she declared she wanted to be with *Il Duce*. Whether an emotional response or fear, she went to the side of Mussolini and this caused both to fall under the volley from the German gun.

After this double execution, the bodies were taken to Milano to be hanged upside down in the large *piazza*. Even as a small girl, I remember thinking of what a terrible scene this must have been, but this was the payment to Mussolini for his alliance to Hitler.

In Italy, after the war, all weapons used in World War II were destroyed, part of the protocol for all war weapons recovered. A recent article in an Italian paper reported that an ex-partisan on his death bed revealed the location of the gun that killed Mussolini.

The gun was recovered in a church and indeed appears to be the same gun used by the partisans. The director of the local museum has begged the authorities to preserve this gun as a museum display and not be destroyed.

39

Arrivederci Fiume

After the war ended, our family as we knew it was gone. Everything was confusing for me, and it seemed that nobody had any idea of what the future would bring. Our pastor came to our home many times to talk to my mother. I don't remember being included in these visits and no explanation of any kind was offered. I had a feeling of great apprehension.

I only knew that some plans were being made and that events beyond my understanding and control were moving quickly. Looking back, I realize now how important it is to include children in family planning, regardless how serious the situation is. I had a feeling of great insecurity and the uncertainty that comes from being surrounded by change with no information available to be able to form an idea of what is happening. I trusted my mother and I knew that she would do what needed to be done, and I never questioned her decision. Deep down, I knew I had to go along with these plans.

My sister and I were suddenly on a train, leaving Fiume for Trieste, our first stop. The pastor, his wife, and three children were also with us. I didn't know where we were all going.

Now I realize that the pastor had arranged for us to be cared for while my mother was in a serious mental condition and could not cope with life. By this time, she knew for a certainty that my brother had been killed. She had no way of knowing if Father was dead or alive, or where he could be. Nobody really knew what happened in the concentration camps, people were in the dark on what was really going on there.

The stop in Trieste was fun. The highlight was to be treated by the GIs to a pastry party for the five of us children, probably arranged by a troop chaplain. The pastor's three children and my sister and I were seated around a table and all the wonderful pastries were passed around American-style in a platter for us to choose from. Soldiers were all around, coming and going. I am sure they had quite a show looking at us. I had never seen anything like it, pastries of different kinds I never tasted before. We each had a little plate and as the tray would go around we chose one to eat, then the tray would be passed again. All the other kids were just eating and ready for the next tray that came around, except me. I was actually hoarding them all in my plate, just waiting for the next tray so I could choose a different one. The pastries were so beautiful and so different. I had no idea how I was going to start eating, but the end of the tray passing came about and then all the other children with their empty plates, started to look at my full plate of pastries. To my surprise, they all came and picked one of the pastries off my plate. They must have thought I could not eat them. I just sat quietly with a long serious face, seeing all my pastries disappear and I knew that it served me right. The lesson was, he who waits too long loses.

The long train ride to Firenze was memorable. All of us five children and other people were crammed together in open cars. There were no bathrooms and we were allowed off the train only on its scheduled stops. I remember we had to relieve ourselves many times on the rail bed either when the train was slow moving or if we had time to step down. Once, when I could not hold it any more, I climbed up boxes to the edge of the train, hanging over the side. We, the children, were not allowed to step far from the train. We were the responsibility of the pastor and we could be left behind at the station. The trip seemed interminable to me with many stops in small towns.

Finally, we arrived in Florence and I was taken to a large house where I would spend the next two years of my childhood. My sister was instead taken to an orphanage near Rome. We both had been sent to the place where the pastor could find room for us. They were children's shelters. The one in Firenze was a center sponsored by the Valedensian Church. In Rome, the area was called E42, with large buildings developed by Mussolini years earlier, then abandoned, and converted in an orphanage.

My sister's place was much worse than mine, as I found out later. There were a lot more children and she contracted lice and all of her thick blonde hair had to be shaved off. She was only seven and the place was very hard for her at such a tender age. She had always been protected by Mother or Dinellis and aunts and uncles. Now she was with a very controlled situation with maybe a hundred children. No personalized care or special attention. She was just another child there. I was somewhat luckier.

40

Life in an Institution

It was called the *collegio*, but also called *orfanatrofio* (orphanage). It might have been a luxury house at one time, but had been donated to the church for charitable purposes. It was located in an affluent residential neighborhood, not far from the center of Firenze. Across the intersection was a park with large beautiful trees. I loved the trees, as I do now, and I felt protected among them when walking to school.

Most of the children were not orphans. Most of them seemed to have relatives or some family that sent them packages. There were fifteen to twenty girls of all ages. The youngest were four and five and the oldest, eighteen. The older girl may have been the daughter of the director of the institution. She had a room of her own. She played the piano skillfully, a result of many lessons, and no doubt came from a family that was better off. I had a feeling that plans for a better life were in store for her. I was about ten and almost every age was represented.

My life here seemed alien to me because I had been accustomed to the freedom of our family on the outskirts of Fiume. I had much anxiety and sadness buried in me with the loss of two brothers, the struggles of our family trying to stay together, my mother absence and father almost considered dead. I became unnaturally quiet and withdrawn among all these girls. It was a foreign country to me here.

I wonder if this is how many children feel when they go to a foster home? Abandoned, at a mercy of strangers, like they don't belong, as if they were in a dream that hopefully will end and they will reunite with their family?

Life here revolved around this new home and the school I attended. We walked to school through the park in a little group and to the street where the public school was located. On the way back to the home, I would see vendors of all kinds on the street with their tables full of either food or objects to sell. My favorite table was where they cooked *castagnata.* It was a pie made of chestnut flour, and it was very delicious to me. When my aunt Irene sent me a little money from Milano, I then could buy a piece.

I don't remember any teachers in particular, I was just a number in the large classroom. One teacher, however, did bring me out of my seat one time by inviting me to the blackboard and asking me to point out the city I came from. This was a different event for the children who lived in this city all their life. My hand pointed to Fiume and a picture was snapped. I was a rarity and incomprehensible to children who stayed with their parents all their life. I was a foreigner who came from a faraway country.

One time while walking from school, I found 500 lira on the street. Of course I went by the rule "finders, keepers" and with that money, I was able to buy for a few days a piece of chestnut pie after school. I was always hungry, that wedge of pie filled the spot.

Occasional trips into the city with the older girls gave me the opportunity to see the cathedral and other points of interest in Florence. But the trips to the dentist, I had to walk all alone. This was my first experience with a dentist.

Shortly after I arrived at the center, the supervisor reported the state of my teeth were in. I had a bad odor and a lot of toothaches. My parents were not available to make decisions, so it was arranged for me to go to the dentist. I was ten years old and I didn't know anything about dentists. All I knew was that I had big holes in my teeth and they had to be pulled out.

I had to make the trip in the streets of Florence a few times because I had more than one tooth to be pulled. I remember being able to put my tongue deep inside a tooth or two, and there was a bad taste in my mouth. The totally decayed teeth were pulled easily without local anesthesia.

I became very fearful of dentists and it was very traumatic to have teeth pulled. At the time I made the assumption that this was normal procedure, or maybe the teeth were so far gone that he did not think anesthesia was necessary. It was still a grisly experience, but perhaps the dentist was giving free services as I had no money to pay for it. During the visits, and while walking to the dentist's office I felt like I was in state of shock all the time. I felt totally alone in the midst of people. I felt almost like I was in a daze.

41

My Life in Firenze

The entrance to the two-story house was a large, heavy double door that entered into a marble atrium or hall. To the right were big rooms with double doors. One led into the dining room, another to a room used for activities such as sewing and embroidery. There was a piano where we gathered around to sing, mostly hymns from our church.

The dining room had a long table and chairs and wooden counters with cabinets below. The activity room had only sparse furniture, mostly chairs and some tables. On a wall, there were small cubicles, similar to lockers, for the children's personal things. To the left of the front entrance was a hallway leading to the kitchen where we were not allowed.

The most impressive part of the entrance hall was the wide marble staircase near the kitchen entrance, leading up to the second floor where it ended on a circular landing opening up to doorways leading to the bedrooms or dormitories. There was one bathroom upstairs and a second smaller bathroom on the first floor which was a long narrow room. Often, we had to wait our turn to use one of the bathrooms and had only a few minutes before somebody would be knocking on the door. We all had to take *olio di merluzzo* (castor oil) on a regular basis.

The upstairs bedrooms had small balconies with French doors, and the iron railing had an elaborate design. Some of the bedrooms faced the street and others overlooked a wonderful garden. Many times, I would come back from school and go hide on the balcony to watch the swallows playing in the sky. I would go to dinner, then come back and watch the sunset with the swallows going back and forth by the balcony. I would cry and cry for the freedom I'd lost, for my mother, my family, my home and my city. My constant thought was my parents and Fiume and how it will be when I return. I would say over and over, "I have to go back to Fiume!" just like in *The Wizard of Oz*. Only I had never heard of Dorothy, and my homecoming never happened, like it did for Dorothy.

I never saw Fiume again, until much later in life and then I could not even find the street where I lived.

42

Via Silvio Pellico

This was the address of the *collegio.* Diagonally from the big house was the *Piazzale D'Azzeglio,* a wonderful little park in the middle of the city. The *collegio* must have been one of the villas at one time, completely enclosed with cement walls and a tall, large iron gate. Here, so many girls of different backgrounds lived under the supervision of two women. We never saw the cook or people working in the kitchen.

The older girls would all stay together as friends. They did not include younger girls in their circle. They seemed to have a lot of things that only they could talk about to each other.

Several times packages would arrive from America. It was a big event. Large boxes of clothes were placed in the main hall and we all were able to find some clothes and shoes that would fit us.

It was so much fun and we all needed clothes badly. I could not believe when I found a pair of shoes that fit me perfectly. I was so happy just to know that somebody else had feet like mine in another part of the world and now I felt lucky to have the shoes.

The clothes I found were the best I ever had and I wondered who could have been the girl of about nine or ten that wore them before. I was so thankful. The clothes were probably collected in churches and organizations to help the people after the war. They were Godsent. I totally wore out the clothes and shoes wearing them every day. Silently, I thanked the person that donated the clothes.

So many times, I thought about how wonderful it was to have these clothes and who could have been wearing them and was my size. I was slightly bigger than most of the other short Italian girls my age. I was sure the girl in America was the same size as me and the same age.

Other times, we had visits from GIs who brought us cookies, candies and gum. We never would have had these treats otherwise. The soldiers seemed to be so happy just seeing us all excited when they came to the home. As children, we were very impressed by them, and I watched them as they would come in all smiling with gifts. I just silently watched men from America, a country I never knew anything about, except from the adventure books I read of Emilio Salgari. For the first time in my life, I saw something very wonderful: a viewer with slides of America! I just clicked the little viewer and another scene would appear on the screen. It was magical for me and it could only come with the *Americans.* This all seemed like another world to me. The magical night lights of cities, streets, and the very tall buildings were astounding to me. The cities were unreal and the scenic areas really did seem from another world.

Most of all, I remember the GI's energy and enthusiasm, their happiness in seeing us happy. I think some of the older girls were even instantly in love with them, flirting with them. I heard them later discuss all the details of the Americans' features and their manners. They acted as if they were in love and they kept their discussion among them excluding the younger kids. I was also curious about the GIs and one of the major things at least I observed was that they were always chewing gum. This seemed kind of cute and very unique because we never heard or seen gum before in our life. This was definitely very American. The visits with the GIs were brief and a good thing or the girls would have really fallen in love followed by disappointments. The girls were only about fourteen or sixteen.

My favorite person at the *collegio* was an Ethiopian girl, about fourteen, named Acquadoro. She was tall and very slim with beautiful features and African hair. She walked like the princess of the Nile, so straight and so proud. When she cut her own hair, I collected it for doll's pillows. I did a lot of hand-sewing for a doll. The cuttings made a very fluffy pillow. Acquadoro was amused and was happy to give me her hair. She didn't talk very much, maybe she didn't know Italian very well, and she had an accent. Acquadoro was very reserved and she appeared mysterious to me. She never talked about her family, but I had a feeling that she could be from a upper-class family, maybe a princess in Ethiopia, the way she was looking down as if we were her subjects. Most of the girls were shorter than she was. Once, when Acquadoro's mother came for a visit from Rome, I could see that she, like her daughter, was very tall and slim, and also very silent. She wore a type of turban and a different style of dresses with fine fabric draped over the shoulders. The mother appeared sad to me, never smiling. I wanted so much to be close and talk to her, as I would have with my own mother, but she moved away every time I tried a friendly gesture.

Many years later, I learned that Acquadoro's mother suffered from tuberculosis and died a few years later. I also found out much later that her daughter also contracted the infection and died of the same disease.

I don't remember the background of the other girls, but I was the only one from far-away Fiume. They were all from the same general area in Tuscany. Their families sent packages and one time I was amazed when the girl said she was eating *ucellini,* which turned out to be some meat folded in a pastry or pasta and baked. This was typical food of the area. All the children were not familiar with the part of Italy I came from, and it was hard for them to understand where the city was located. They sensed that my family was too far away to send any food packages.

Even though we had three meals a day, I was always hungry. In between meals, my stomach was growling. One Sunday after church, I saw the helpers bring in the spaghetti and sauce and place it on the counter in the dining room. Dinner was not being called, and I kept peeking through the crack in the door and smelling the delicious food. The doors were closed, the room was dark, all the shutters were closed, and everybody was in the activity room. While all the others were occupied, I sneaked out and slipped into the dining room. I was the most hungry girl there, because I did not have packages of food and goodies as the other girls did. Their little lockers were packed with goods that they could nibble on between meals.

The spaghetti sauce was in a separate dish in the dark dining room buffet. I speculated how I could get a taste of it and then I put my fingers in the bowl. Just at the moment, the director, a tough and imposing woman, came in, turning the lights on. I hid my hands behind my back, but she was furious and ordered, "Show me your hand!" I slowly brought my hands in front of me, one covered with sauce. Then there was a severe scolding and punishment in the corner of the room. Also, part of my meal was taken away. I was very ashamed and upset for what I had done. It was very embarrassing for a while, but children forget easily.

Another day, after I had committed this crime, another incident occurred in which I acquitted myself more favorably. The director announced, *Il Recovero dei Vecchi* (the old folk's home) has invited two of our girls to spend Sunday and have dinner with them.

All the girls started talking at the same time. One would say, "I am not going to be with those old people." Another, "They have big noses and no teeth." They scorned the idea, giggling and making fun of the oldsters. I felt sad for the old people who were probably looking forward to see children and young people. Their feelings would be hurt if nobody came to their Sunday dinner.

At the risk of ridicule, I suddenly found my voice: "I will go!"

The other girls made fun of me as I had expected, talking with a voice of old people and mimicking them in gestures: bent over, making terrible faces. I was the only one going to the home. Nobody else would venture with me, not even for moral support. They all thought this was an event they had no desire to go to, or please anyone at all.

As it turned out, when I got to the home, the old people were so happy and they treated me like a special guest. After the wonderful dinner, which I felt fortunate to have, they had a little program and at the end of it all they nominated me *Reginetta dei Vecchi.* There was a trend to nominate a queen of "something" as it is today, such as, Daffodil Queen. I was indeed the little queen of the day, a ten-year-old who won a popularity contest among the sweet old people of the home. I came back to the *collegio* with many little gifts: coloring books, pencils, and even some clothes they had bought with their little money to present to the girls from the orphanage! I was happy. It was a wonderful day and so much fun. After all, I was there to get all the attention from at least twenty people, all trying to hug me and love me. When I came back to the *collegio*, I actually acted like a queen, with all my gifts to show. I felt exuberant, a contrast to my usual serious manner. I won a contest and I had no other contestant to question it! I was after all the *Regina dei Vecchi*.

The only other time I felt so happy and lucky was with the occasional packages from my Aunt Irene from Milano and the packages from America.

There were some happy times in Florence such as these and it made life a little more bearable for the two years I was there.

43

The Vacation

The girls at the orphanage were allowed to leave on summer vacation if they had relatives or friends they could visit. My mother was still in Fiume and healing from a breakdown. My father was still missing in Germany, so I had no place to go.

Some families affiliated with the church volunteered to care for those of us in such circumstances. One family that lived on a farm near Siena, *un podere,* usually run by the owners with *contadini* doing most of the work, invited Acquadoro and me. We were about the only ones who didn't have any place to go when school was out. I am sure the *dirretrice* herself wanted to take a vacation. So, we were taken to the farm to spend some time with this family.

I was about ten years old by then and my recollections of details are hazy. I knew that I had no family to support me or any other plans and I was being farmed out. My Aunt Irene in Milano was the only one interested in my welfare, but she was very young and trying to support herself with very little money and no home of her own. She lived with the family she worked for.

However, I was excited and looking forward to a new adventure in the country. I was grateful that a family was willing to take us for a few weeks in the summer.

I remember a farmhouse on top of a hill surrounded by barns and storage sheds. As in medieval days, most of the farms houses were on top of a hill and the fields below were very visible at all angles from the top.

There was a vineyard on the hillside and fields of other crops and numerous fruit trees. Closer to the house, there were vegetables and flower beds, and dozens of chickens were running free all over.

One afternoon after the midday meal, I started to explore. I was all alone and it was very quiet and very hot. This was a time of siesta for the farmers. I entered the dark entrance to a big barn. When my eyes adjusted to the gloom, I could see a dirt floor covered with straw. In the middle of this scene were several large buckets covered with a fine white mesh. It seemed very mysterious. There was a pleasant fragrance in the barn. There were at least twelve or more of these buckets, and they were placed in an orderly manner. It made me think something very important was hiding in them.

After cautiously walking around to see what else could be happening in this dark place, I went to one of the buckets. I lifted the mesh and there was gold! It was so yellow and smooth, it might have been gold dust. The buckets were filled with golden honey! I started eating it, dipping my finger in the gold and I ate as much as I could, then I replaced the mesh and planned to return the next day. What a windfall! I never seemed to get enough to eat and the honey gave me a lot of energy. The farmers would never miss the little that I ate.

The following afternoon was again very quiet and still hot, so I headed again for the honey barn. I never even started to eat any of the honey when I heard a voice from far away. There was a stillness in the huge windowless building. I listened carefully. The voice was faint, as if from far away, but I could hear my name barely, then a little more clearer, "Leda, Leda!"

During the war, I was able to hear the planes long before anybody else. This time, I could hear the voice. I knew it was there and I would be the only person able to hear it. I finally could hear a word not clearly. It was my name, which no one else I ever knew had it. It was a rare name in Italy, unknown except in mythology. It could only be one person calling my name.

I thought I was imagining. Then the voice came nearer, and finally I knew it was my mother! She had started calling from way down at the bottom of the hillside. As she climbed the long, winding road to the farm she kept calling my name. When I finally was certain it was my mother, I ran down the hill and around the bend of the road where I found her with tears in her eyes. My mother had finally come to bring me home!

She had gone to Firenze where she was told I was at this distant farm. She had traveled two or three days from the coast of Yugoslavia to Firenze, then Siena, and then into the countryside. She had to take several trains and walked long distances between railroad stations. All the time trying to find this farm which was not near any village. But then we would have found each other no matter what, such was our secret link that nothing could really separate us.

44

Zia Irene

When I was in Florence, my auntie was one of my consolations. She made me feel like I was not abandoned, she sent me a package whenever she could. I treasured the little gifts of colored pencils. It was at this time that I drew a golden retriever which she kept throughout her life, as I found out later.

The word for aunt is *zia* in the Italian language. Zia Irene was our closest, most beloved aunt. Zia was born on December 4, 1911, in Fiume, now Croatia. She was in her early twenties when I was born, while my mother was in her forties. She was the last surviving child of Maria (Balogh) and Pali Soltesz. Another child followed her, Arpad, but he died in his third year. Her father disappeared during WWI. The two youngest children, Irene and Emilia, had to go to an orphanage while the older children had to find work to support the remaining family.

Zia Irene was a very sensitive child and was totally ignored by her mother, who, as I remember, was not a verbal person and was without affection. Whether because of the language barrier, overwhelming difficulties, or by her very nature, she was distant and disconnected, totally uncommunicative. As a little girl, I remember wondering if it was because we were girls and not boys.

The family moved from Hungary to Fiume, the Austro-Hungarian port, in hopes of immigrating to the United States where Maria Balogh's brothers lived, in Chicago. These brothers had sent money for the trip. One of the stories I had heard was that all of the money was eventually lost in gambling by their father, my grandfather, Pali Soltesz.

After the orphanage, Zia Irene went to work for a rich family in Milano. She did all of the shopping, cleaning and errands that were requested. The family treated her well, even as their own daughter, but she was at their disposal for all of their needs. Even though she was not living her own life, she did not mind. Maybe because she had some other special people she lived for once or twice a year. My mother, Yolanda, was very close to her, so her children became Zia Irene's children. As the oldest sister, sixteen-years older, my mother had been everything for her in her childhood, the nourishing love which was missing even from her own mother, then at a young age in an orphanage.

It is hard to describe this amazing person, Zia Irene. I remember my Aunt Irene vividly, from the time I was three or four. At that time, she lived in Milano and was working for a family of Russian nobility who were fugitives from the October Revolution. She was dedicated to this family too, but again, there was no opportunity for her own education or personal enrichment. The best years of her life were given to this family, who became dependent on her for all their needs. She never married. Later, she told me there was one opportunity but it did not work out. Zia Irene's youth must have been very sad. She had told me once how she would watch the city at night from her window and would cry. She said she did not know why, but I know that she was crying for a life that she was missing. She never talked about her past, but this was a moment of togetherness we shared later in life.

As a little girl, I looked forward to her visits. Aunt Irene knew exactly what to bring us; the special clothing that could only come from Milano. She would bring dolls that we would not have had otherwise. Zia Irene was a wonderful gift to us. She loved our family so much. Her visits from Milano to Fiume, near Trieste, were special. For days, we would talk about her coming. Aunt Irene took all the pictures we have of our childhood, otherwise we would not have had any photos. She was the only one that had a camera, I supposed because she was from Milano. With our family of four children, our parents were overtaxed and had no time or money for cameras or store-bought clothes and toys. My mother made all our clothes on her prized Singer sewing machine. Not many people had that either, they sewed by hand.

Aunt Irene would have made a wonderful mother, but she lived for and shared with my mother. Later in life, she became our mother when my mother died in 1957.

WWII interrupted the visits and our happy life. Even then, though there were hard times, there were always packages. After the war when I was in an orphanage in Florence for two years. I remember receiving some wonderful packages from Aunt Irene. I used to wonder how she could guess exactly what I needed most: underwear, and such things as colored pencils and drawing paper, I used to love to draw. Years later I found, pinned to the wall of her apartment, a drawing I had made of a golden retriever.

Zia Irene made it possible for my sister and me to come to this country by taking care of the paperwork my parents could not do. They could not bring themselves to fill out papers to relinquish their only two remaining children. She knew in her heart that this was in our best interest, even though the laws would not allow her to come with us because of her Hungarian citizenship. She would not be able to be close to us. Another immigration quota allowed her to go only to Canada. She lived here for a few years and worked toward receiving her GED and then become a Licensed Practical Nurse. She loved her work in the hospital in Toronto. Her adjustment to the new world was much more difficult than ours because she was older.

Later, because of the love she had for us, she left Canada and all her friends and obtained a job at Virginia Mason Hospital in Seattle so she could be close to us while we lived in Tacoma.

As a nurse who loved her work, her world was all about people. In her private life, she cared for the ill and lonely and for all the people with whom she came in contact throughout her life. She was also an artist and her paintings were another expression of her life. She would give her paintings to people that asked for them. She encouraged other artists and influenced them in doing good work. Zia had a generous spirit and with her modest earnings, still gave to the needy. She was a rescuer of stray cats and even birds that came to her windowsill. Most of all, she was always there for my sister and me.

45
Villa Vittoria

Eventually, my father returned from Germany. He walked almost all the way from the prison camp to Fiume and the journey was a difficult two months. Rides from occasional military vehicle and freight trains were of short distances, traveling within Germany, and most of the time, he was on foot.

When he finally arrived, he was a skeleton, having had little food along the way. This was 1946 and I was in Firenze at this time. He and Mother started to put their lives together. They, as well as hundreds of other families, made plans to leave Fiume, for political reasons. Fiume became part of Yugoslavia under the regime of the dictator Tito. My father and brother had not suffered and fought for a dictator. Houses were taken over as property of the state and people were forced to abandon their Italian citizenship. The Italian language was no longer to be used in the schools, or for official matters. Anybody who stayed had to accept Yugoslavian citizenship and give up many freedoms they were used to. The emigration process was underway soon after the war ended and our families became scattered.

Uncle Alika and his family went to Bolzano, where he was able to open his own barber shop. Aunt Emilia, with her husband and son, also went to Bolzano where she found a job at the post office. Aunt Elena, with her husband and son, went to Marghera, near Venice, where the husband found work in a factory. Uncle Paolo went to Rome with his wife, where he was employed as a caretaker in the large Valdensian Church. His grown son, with wife and child, went to Milano with opportunity to work there. My father and mother went to Pinerolo, near Torino, where my father could use his shipyard skills in a foundry. The arrangement for our family and Uncle Paolo's family were made by Pastor Guy of our Church in Fiume, the same man who had provided for my sister and me right after the war when my father was still missing. Aunt Irene was in Milano also where she lived most of her adult life.

My Uncle Pepi, from my father's side of the family, moved to New Zealand with his wife. My father's sisters, Aunt Zinka, widowed a few years, with her two children and Aunt Milka, stayed in Split, Dalmatia, where they had already been living for many years.

Shortly after his return from Germany, my father left for Pinerolo to locate a place for us to live. He found a farmhouse where our former neighbors from Fiume, the Dinellis, were already settled.

At this point, my sister and I returned from our orphanages. We had been gone two years. In fact in my case, I had completely lost the accent of our native city and was then speaking as a Florentine. Mother could not help laugh when she heard me talk with a strange Italian accent.

As in time of disaster, people offered housing as well as they could. I'm sure this farmhouse was not in use at this time, but was then rented to people coming into the area. This was a typical two-story house where only the upstairs was used and the downstairs was only storage and animal shelter. The upstairs farmhouse was divided into two separate places sharing one bathroom.

My mother was not happy with this arrangement for some reason even though we had been good neighbors before. As she did with all her concerns, she went to Pastor

Guy, who was also a refugee from Fiume, now assigned to the Valdensian Church in Torino. Thinking back, I believe she wanted to be isolated from the togetherness of our previous life, to find peace for her soul.

The region of Piemonte has the largest population of Valdensians in Italy, and the rest of Italy may not even know this fact. In those days Catholic Italians did not understand any other religion, except in this particular area of Italy. There had been some persecutions of the Valdensians, in past history in this region. Many hundred of years before the Valdensian had come to these Alps refuge to practice their religion. The Waldenses, or *Valdesi* as in Italian, were the first believers in freedom.

Pastor Guy was able to find a space in an old villa which had not been used during the war years, a few miles from Pinerolo, almost in the mountains.

In normal times, *Villa Vittoria* most likely had been used as a vacation summer place, while at other times its owner lived in the city. In Italy, it is customary for any wealthy family to have a retreat in the mountains or the shore. Italians usually take all of August for vacation as well as the usual holidays.

This villa was located on a hilltop on the road to Sestriere, an alpine ski area. Below the villa was a small village named Riaglietto. A little dirt road not far from the village led us past an old flour mill where the wheel still turned in the small river coming down from the mountains. Past the mill, the road crossed over a wooden bridge before coming to the large iron gates of the villa. After entering the gates between large concrete columns to hold the heavy iron, we entered in the road belonging to the villa property. This road became steep shortly after the entrance, with only two concrete strips for the wheels of a car. This road of about one-half a block led to a large four-car garage: a concrete structure with a roof serving as a terrace surrounded by railing. The view from the terrace to the valley below and the mountains in the background was spectacular.

Another stairway from the terrace went farther up to a higher level of small terraces, the larger one being on top of the garage then gradually up the hill with steps to the much smaller areas opposite to each other, offering more views of the countryside. After this garage area and all the different levels, there was a short steep path to concrete steps ending at a level garden in front of the house entrance.

This formal garden in front of the house had been neglected to a point where flower beds were no longer visible. The grass had taken over and was high and brown. In the middle of the garden, there was a pond with scarce lily pads and a dry fountain with a crumbling concrete statue of a woman holding a vase. There was barely any water at the bottom of the little concrete pond. There was another concrete terrace near this pond overlooking the valley, but overgrown trees were obstructing most of it. There was fruit trees but the only one producing fruit was a persimmony. In the summer, it was loaded with wonderful large fruit, ripened on the vine.

It must have been truly a paradise in better times.

The house was a three-story house designed for a single family. At ground level was a small separate apartment where the middle-aged caretakers lived: a couple with no children. On the other side of their quarters was the kitchen for the villa's owners with a circular stairway leading up to the dining room. I could imagine servants that came up with their dishes of food.

On the main level of the house, from the garden leading to the double-door entrance, one entered into a large round hall. On the right were locked rooms where the owners had stored their possessions. On the left of the hall were our family quarters. At the center of the hall, there was a marble staircase leading upstairs to the third level. On this floor were bedroom and the only bathroom, and a small kitchen. This space was already occupied by another refuge family, a mother and her grown son had been placed there by Pastor Guy before we arrived.

Our assigned area consisted of a single large room, at one time the dining room. The room had two French doors opening into a spacious sunroom: a glass enclosed veranda that wrapped around two sides of the house in L-shape. At the northern end of the veranda there was an ornate billiard table. This area was facing the back garden, the grotto, and the forest in the back of the house.

At one end of the dining room was an iron spiral staircase leading down to a kitchen in the basement, adjacent to the caretaker's quarters. They had their own kitchen and bathroom.

With no bathroom in our own place, my father had to improvise an outhouse, a privy in the yard. We made the best of it.

Villa Vittoria, as I understood, belonged to a well-to-do family that had not been able to use it because of war shortages. It had been empty and virtually abandoned for years. The caretakers had been left as guards but had not maintained the property. There was a vineyard below the house tended by a farmer, but during the times he worked in the vineyard he never talked to us or anybody else. It was well taken care of, however, and the grapes were growing well.

The years of neglect showed in the interior of the house as well as the gardens outside. I could only imagine how it must have been! The veranda glass (sunroom) was leaking here and there, the kitchen was very dark with old paint and poor lighting.

There was a mysterious grotto in the fir trees and the large magnolias in the back of the house. As I walked to the grotto I could smell the wonderful fragrance of the magnolias in bloom. I could also stand in the sunroom, very close to the giant, white blossoms. The magnolia tree was shading the pool table area. It seemed all planned: people could play pool and drink the essence of the fragrant, beautiful flowers.

The grotto was a rough, manmade cave, big enough for several people to enter. The story was that the owners of the villa during the affluent years had large parties. The grounds were full of surprises: hidden paths, an old stone staircase to the forest above, large open areas in the trees where games were played. One tale was of how the host would invite guests to the grotto for wine tasting, then he would turn a secret switch which would release a fine spray of water to catch the unsuspecting.

The forest above the grotto could be reached by a long narrow, cobblestone stair that was covered with ivy and surrounded by tall pines and firs. Here and there, fragrant violets and cyclamens, were scattered among the trees.

The villa truly was a rich playground, but not for us!

While growing up we had been accustomed to a nice home. Now, in our early teens we had to live in condition below our previous standards, where we had marble floors and a beautiful bathroom. Here, we had no room of our own, we were lucky to still have a few pieces of our furniture brought from Fiume. The few pieces of our modern furniture were still in original shape with my mother's care.

We really had no clothes to wear to school, growing out of any clothes we had, we could not buy new ones. I had to watch my mother sinking deeper and deeper into depression. I implored her and she promised to make new skirts out of other clothes, but she could not get organized to do it. I was persistent and stubborn, asking her to make clothes for us, not able to understand why she could not. She did not let her feelings be known and could only retaliate by becoming angry. She used to love sewing and was proud of her Singer sewing machine, one of the items she could not part with the move. I had to wear the same skirt and blouse to school every day, and the other girls noticed it. I always had pretty clothes my mother made when I was little, with colorful aprons to keep them clean. Now, I was twelve and thirteen years old and felt embarrassed for so many things.

In the winter, in this villa, we had to scrounge for firewood for the only heat we had from an old clay stove that was very inefficient. Sometimes, it was very difficult to find wood in the snow. When spring came, my mother spent all her time in the garden, now converted to vegetables. Many times, I would start making soup because my mother would not come in until late at night, and we were hungry. It seemed she existed on coffee and some bread. Father was in the sanitarium during this time, so it was just the three of us, mother, sister and I.

One summer day, I talked my sister into going to the orchard of the farms on the hillside where there were fruit trees. In the midday, the farmers were resting, so we climbed over the fences and found ourselves in the midst of an apple and pear orchard. We started filling our gathered cotton skirts with fruit and we thought we were safe as the farmers don't start working the fields again until later afternoon. Instead, a red-faced *contadina* came running and yelling after us. We ran down a dry creek bed to escape, but my sister froze in fear and could not run. I had to go back and pull her until she could walk, but then she would stop again, frightened. We finally made our way back over the fence and hoped the farmer woman didn't know who the thieves were.

Years later when I visited Italy with my teenage sons, I walked to the edge of this farm and behold, the same *contadina* with the same red apron came out! I said, "You don't know me, but I remember you!" She smiled and said, "Yes, I do remember you and your sister. It is good to see you!"

The village of Riaglietto was a small group of houses with one store, on the road to Sestriere. Surrounding the village were scattered fields and farmhouses inhabited by families who had lived there for generations. When they saw us at the store, they stared as people do with strangers in their midst. In bigger towns, it is not quite as noticeable. I remember going to the store to buy sugar or flour or some other item, and having to ask to put the bill on the account because we didn't have money. I detected annoyance on the face of the store lady. There is no kindness when it comes to money. We would always pay our small account later, when Pastor Guy would help us financially. My father, in TB sanitarium, was helpless with his illness already gone too far. There was no such thing as public assistance then, or any welfare agency. It was all up to us. We lived off our garden for the most part, or bartered items with farmers nearby. Mother would wash clothes in exchange and was willing to do anything, but people did not help as much and could not see our situation because they never had been themselves in it. They had their farms, their homes, they had each other, and we had no one and nothing much.

We lived at the villa long enough to experience two summers and one winter. My sister and I went to Pinerolo to school and at the beginning my father worked at the local foundry. We traveled every day on a train from

Riaglietto to Pinerolo, a much bigger city. These hard times were when my father could no longer work after discovery of tuberculosis.

When we first moved to the villa, my mother, as was her habit, spent hours in the garden of the villa. She salvaged some roses and peonies that had been long abandoned and completely relandscaped the garden. She cleaned the debris from the pond and restored it by adding water from the well. In fact, all our water came from the well. She planted vegetables so that we always had enough to make soups and vegetable dishes. We also had rabbits and chickens. One big white rabbit was our pet and roaming free in the garden. We also had Lilli, a cat who had at least three litters, which we could not even feed or give away. We had a small Shelty that my father brought home after work. Then we could take care of him, his name was Mucchi. Later we had hard times, but these animals were very special, especially for my mother.

There was a well outside, but only running water was in the kitchen sink. My mother had to do the washing in the sink, then put the clean washing in buckets and carry them to the river for rinsing. We could not use all the water from the sink. The little river that came down from the mountains to the old mill passed near the villa property. We carried the heavy buckets of washing across a trail to reach the river.

Summers were warm and beautiful. The only sadness was watching my mother working in the garden, hour after hour, forgetting about us and the meals that needed to be prepared. She was probably thinking of what life had done to her family and the two sons that were lost. Often I saw her trying to hide tears while working with her head low in the flowers and vegetables. Maybe she even knew then she would lose us too.

Winters were cold in this region, with lots of snow. This was a ski country and from high on the villa, I could watch the streams of cars, skis on top, headed for Sestriere. I said to myself, *Some day I too will ski!*

Our life at *Villa Vittoria* ended in less than two years after the tuberculosis was discovered and my father left for the sanitarium. Nothing had been stable for us after the war, but I didn't know our life together would also end.

46
Agape

We started to go to the Valdensian Church in Pinerolo as we did in Fiume. Mother wanted us to go even when she couldn't go. It was a tough trip, a lot of walking and a train to get there. We'd go down the hill from the old villa, to catch the little train at the village at the right time, then it was about forty five minutes on the train to Pinerolo. In this town, we had a little more walking to do as the church was not near the train. With her poor legs and now I know, her sick heart, she stayed at home a lot more. She wanted to be left alone it appeared to me, while my father was away in the sanitarium.

We went with the young people's group and joined some of the activities. One, time a trip was arranged to go to Agape, a village in the mountains built by the Valdensians after the war. It was still under construction, with cabins for summer camps and for group activities. It was a pretty setting at the base of a mountain in the Alps, not far from Pinerolo. Our pastor from Fiume was settled there, working with his whole family.

This time I remember mostly Kari, a Norwegian girl. Kari was about my age twelve or thirteen, but ages ahead of me. She was beautiful, a typical Norwegian developed like an eighteen-year-old. Her father worked in Italy in a company that may have had ties with Norway. They were well off, with expensive cars. Her thick blonde hair was usually combed in two long braids. She was very tall, certainly unlike any of us. Her round face was white and rosy, and dazzling blue eyes. She wore very snazzy clothes, very tight and short, either skirt or shorts. She had a leather jacket. She was not slim, but she looked very attractive in her stylish clothes.

Kari's statuesque body attracted the older and good-looking boys. The blue of her eyes were paralyzing, with an impish look. On one hike, we reached an empty cabin. We all sat around the benches outside. In the group, there was a very good-looking, tall Italian boy, Roberto. Kari and the older boy went inside. When they came out, we asked: "What is in there?" They laughed and said there was nothing, exchanging glances. None of us understood anything, but after that they were together often.

Agape was a special village where young people worked together to build it. It was a popular place to go for families and children's camps, just for the members of the church.

Much later, I found out that that is where Aquadoro died. She had been working in that village. She was my favorite person at the orphanage in Florence, owned by the Valdensian Church. I remember how often I would watch her and her mother when she spent time there. I felt very sad, feeling that it was not the way I wanted to find her. I really felt so sad because her mother had also died a few years earlier. I was thinking of them away from their country, Ethiopia, and with no one but each other. Aquadoro's mother was not one to become friends with anyone, and she had a look of desperation which she would not share with anyone. Her anguish was locked within. Aquadoro was more sociable but still regarded us as strangers. She was amazed at my interest in her. I watched when she cut her own frizzy hair. It was the first time for me to see an African person. I seemed to sense that they would not adjust and survive in such a different world. This was the reason why of all the girls of the orphanage, Aquadoro was the only one I was seeking to find, later. I had to find her, and then rest in the finality of her fate.

47

Food for Thought

This was the time that I thought we would be a normal family in Villa Vittoria, school, home, our family reunited. It was one of our most difficult times. I was in the early teens and my sister, two years younger, appeared oblivious to our predicament, although I knew she was aware but unable to really believe it.

Today, thinking back, I can relate to the teenage years with today's young people. These years were difficult as they are today. I did want to blend in school, wanted to have normal clothes, more similar to other girls. It's the same today. I was very self-conscious and also very hard on my mother, sometimes even yelling and talking badly to her. I was wearing clothes made from other clothes that my mother sewed on the sewing machine. I wore the same blouse and skirt every day. I could not accept the fact that we did not have any money to buy anything, even food. Certainly not fabric to make clothes. No income in the family. Yet I wanted to blame my parents for our situation. Maybe children do this until they mature and understand better. In my case, I felt I was doing everything, helping washing clothes, then folding them and cooking. I just wanted Mother to sew up something for me to go to school. I expected too much, maybe she did not have enough material anyway when she had taken apart some other garment.

This was one part of that difficult teenage transition.

On the other hand, I could see how much Mother was suffering.

When we were in the kitchen and there was no visible food preparation, I would start a soup with the vegetable from our garden. Mother always had things growing in every corner of the yard. She loved to grow things and maybe this was her only comfort. Mother would be there and lost in her helplessness would say, "If I only had flour and other ingredients I would make so many good things for you."

My father, always the optimist, once, later, not in these sad times, told me a story I always remember. "There was one hobo who started to make a soup on the open fire. He started the soup with a large rock boiling in the water, pretending it was a soup bone. Others would stop by and make fun of it, but felt bad for him even while they ridiculed him. Then one by one they started to bring an onion, potatoes, and other food. By the end of all the cooking, he had a great soup and they all gathered and had a good meal."

Recently, I was on a trip to Europe. I realized how important food is to most people, and for me, it is only to nourish the body the best way possible an then be thankful.

Talk centered much of the time around places to eat and dishes comparing food and just discussing the meals. On this trip, dinner hour was late in the evening lasting two to three hours with at least three courses.

I know it was not this way for us in Villa Vittoria, because we had homework and then to get up early for school. We had only one dish, polenta and tomato sauce with some meat or just vegetables cooked with potatoes or *capusta* cabbage and noodles.

We also had one small dog, a Shelty, named after a famous dog, Mucchi, and a cat, Lilly, to feed. For the rabbits, my sister and I would go in the valley below and gather grass and clover for them.

My memory goes back to Fiume when mother was

cooking all the good food and special foods for different occasions. At Easter, she made the traditional sweet bread, breaded with a boiled egg in the middle. At Christmas all the sweet rolls made with nuts. All our meals were very tasty, with meat and sauces. She used a lot of paprika as Hungarians do. She loved to cook and make us happy. This is what I'll remember most: food was happiness, because it was shared with love.

48

The Decision

In 1948, my parents moved from Fiume to Pinerolo. At this time, both my sister and I came back from the orphanages, where we were placed after the war (1945). My mother came to the little farm where I was staying for the summer near Siena and brought me back to Pinerolo. My sister was already home from the orphanage. Mother had traveled by train and bus to this farm after finding out in Florence that I was staying with a farm family for the summer. Mother was so anxious to see me that she started calling me from the bottom of the hill, "Leda! Leda!" The farm was on top of a Tuscany hill with a long winding road leading to it. I had been much in the dark about my parents immediately after the war when I left Fiume, so I did not expect them. I only remember letters or packages from my Aunt Irene in Florence, but as soon as I heard my name, I knew it was my mother. I abandoned any plans, abandoned to forage into the barn, and started running down the hill. We hugged in tears and joy, looking at each other for a long time. She looked the same almost, except for the gray hair in a bun, dressed in black, eyes deeper now, she had lost weight. Mother only wanted to know about me and told me nothing of what happened after I left Fiume. I learned facts from other people much later.

After this reunion when we were trying to become somewhat settled in Villa Vittoria, it was discovered that my father had contracted tuberculosis in the prison camp and was ordered to a sanitarium in the mountains.

My Aunt Irene felt stranded in Milano. She had a job but no particular attachment to anyone there. She had always been part of our family, and my mother wanted to make her feel that we were like children of her own, as she had done. She continued to visit often here in Piemonte and became even closer in discussing our future. My parents and my aunt knew that my sister and I had a poor chance to get a start in life with my father unable to support us for an indefinite period. We were actually almost foreigners here, where families were there for generations and had their history together.

The three discussed together all the pros and cons of young girls emigrating alone as displaced persons to the USA. We had the political status because Fiume had become part of Yugoslavia after the war and the majority of the citizens became *profughi* and left the area.

This meant again separating our family and depriving our parents of their two remaining children. I know that my mother and father ached at the thought of losing us. Aunt Irene helped them make the decision. "I will go with them! I will emigrate too!"

This was some consolation, at least for the moment. My mother always strong and brave and my father was always an optimist. Their philosophy might as well have been: "Life is either a daring adventure, or nothing." The decision was made with their firm thought that they would follow us as soon as my father was declared cured of TB.

In 1950, all our papers were in progress for my sister, I, and my aunt to emigrate. This required several months in a refugee camp in Bagnoli near Napoli. Bagnoli was a very small town where the Americans and other countries had established a processing center in the old barracks of the Italian Army. We were kept busy with the bureaucratic procedures and didn't see much of anything outside the camp, but watched with great interest the baseball games played by the American occupational forces.

The camp was very large with hundreds of refugees and we lost track of Aunt Irene. She was being processed in a different group, as she was an adult and considered Hungarian even though she lived most of her life in Italy, but we were confident she would be leaving at the same time.

As it turned out, Aunt Irene was not able to qualify for the USA quota and instead was sent to Canada, in Toronto. We actually didn't know much of what was happening, till much later, when we were in the USA. My parents thought she would still be near us, so did we, not realizing how vast the distances are in the two countries. It was good that they didn't know, and they were not even aware of the great distances between the cities in Canada and the cities in USA.

Finally my sister and I were on a train to the port of Bremen, Germany. The parting was very sad. Our little family gathered at the train station in Torino. We spent a very short difficult time together, then the train was leaving with my sister and I leaning out the window, waving good-bye. *"Arrivederci!"* We called until I could only see my parents as two tiny dots on the platform. When the train started moving, they walked slowly alongside, then as fast as they could, along with the train, until my father slowed, trying to prevent some agony, but my mother kept going. Finally, I saw her faltering and reaching for a bench. She sat down, my father now near her, she leaned her head on his shoulder, while he put his arms around her. Both with their white hankies to their eyes, their heads no longer holding up with courage.

49
Un Sogno (A Dream)

"*La vita é un sogno sfuggente*" (Life is a fleeting dream), my mother wrote in my remembrance book, adding to my schoolmates parting words at the end of the school year.

She had said this other times to me as if she meant that life can slip away quickly like a dream, and in the morning, is gone.

The last seven years of her life were sad and difficult. My sister and I, her only remaining children, were gone from her life like a dream.

So often I had heard my mother singing in the happy years and also in the sad years later, songs from the operas. Often I heard: "*Un bel di vedremo*" from *Madame Butterfly* and arias from *Traviata, La Boheme* and *la Forza del Destino*. I had a feeling that she sang to reflect her life. After the war I heard more haunting and sad songs as if she were waiting in vain like Cio-Cio-San.

My mother had a premonition of sorrowful times ahead. That turned out to be true.

In 1948–49, shortly after our family was reunited, it became evident that our life was not going well. We had left Fiume, our hometown, which was taken over by Tito's Yugoslavia, and had come to a little village near Torino. Our faithful pastor found housing for us through friends, and a job for my father. Before the war, my father was a specialized foundry worker in the shipyard, he was one of builders of the twin ships Saturnia and Vulacania. Now he started working in a foundry again.

Father commuted to his job early in the morning and came home late at night. He was always cheerful and happy to have a job. The old villa where we lived was lovely in many ways but the steep walk up to it left my father short of breath. He was exhausted when he came home and he started coughing more and more. A doctor's physical examination revealed tuberculosis, probably acquired in concentration camps. Even in this state, he continued to be the optimist and wrote in my book: *"la vita cominicia domani"* ("Life begins tomorrow"), and what he meant is that there is always a tomorrow. While he was comforting, my mother had a sense of quiet prophecy. She was always right, I knew. Maybe time does not mean anything. Only we realize this just when time is almost gone. A lifetime may be really just an instant. When a person is dying, it has been reported they see their whole lifetime on a screen in a brief moment.

Of course, we all had to commute from the village of Riaglietto to the more distant city of Pinerolo to school or bigger stores or even a movie. Here is when I remember going to my first movie with my mother, probably to escape the world of sadness that now was with her all the time. It was *The Baron of Minchausen*, and another, *The Thief of Bagdad*. I will always remember them.

We were happy to have a home, and I remember well the series of terraces of the villa on top of the garage and gardener quarters. The cement was cracked in many places showing the neglect of time. We rested here after the long hill, and before tackling the second little hill to the house. I loved the view of the vineyards and the valley below. I visualized potted geraniums on the balconies, absent now with the villa abandoned.

Our life took a major change again. My father had to go to a mountain sanitarium, the expected cure of those days.

Mother was left with two daughters and very little money. There was no potential job for her and there was no such thing as public assistance. The life ahead did not look good. Our parents always wanted us to have an education or a trade so we could have a job. Now it was impossible, with my father unable to work. After public elementary schools, in Italy, there are only tuition schools and there was no money for that.

There were a few trips in the mountain sanitarium to visit, and Mother and Father would walk together discussing, while we would go pick flowers in the hills.

We had the option to emigrate to any of the agreed countries (United States, New Zealand, Australia) but not as a family, with my father's condition. Our parents made the supreme sacrifice; to let my sister and me emigrate to the United States, this way giving us a chance to go to school and have a better life. Our life together was coming to an end. My mother sang the songs of doom for her, like Butterfly giving up her child. She had always lived giving her whole self to the family, now everything had to be given up and her future was inescapable sadness.

Our last weeks and days in old Villa Vittoria were days of silent desperation, where my mother said very little to avoid crying in front of us. She would hide her face from us by working in the garden for long periods of hours, never looking up. I knew her tears were falling on the ground where she was working. *Grandi dolori sono muti.* ("Big pain is mute.") She was lost in a world of deep sadness, forgetting even to make meals and she only drank coffee and some bread to fill her stomach. I had taken over in the kitchen, making mostly soups from our vegetable garden. She had only lived for her children and the family, and now everything had to be given up. She lived with her songs that kept her breathing a little longer. Her silence would only escape in her singing all the arias she knew so well. She sang with all her heart in the kitchen, and I could hear her upstairs and outside in the garden. Her beautiful voice floating in the air and embracing me wherever I was, while I studied for exams, or taking care of chores.

My father's philosophy sustained her. He never gave up hope and tried to be cheerful, while mother was unable to accept our parting and think of a possible reunion later. She seemed to know in her heart that she would never see us again.

Then we were on a train in Torino, leaning out the window. Mother and Father were on the platform walking following the train as we were leaving. There was only silence now and many tears. My mother's heart broken, life taken away from her.

At the sanitarium, my father had to have lung surgery. Mother remained alone for two years. She would limp down and up the steep hill to the village to get the mail. After we left the dream of reuniting with us kept her alive for seven years, then her heart gave out. Father died ten years later almost the same time of year. He was able to emigrate shortly after my mother died. He shared his life with my sister and I for ten years. His words are still with me, "Laugh, life is short, don't be mad."

He was right. There is always a new day. "Life begins again tomorrow!"

50
Good-bye *Italia, Arrivederci!*

Near Naples was a large refugee center, where Americans and other countries, like Australia and New Zealand, were processing papers for immigration. We were involved with the American offices. We had one interview, where they were asking us: "How come you are going without your parents? Why, and how do you feel about this, can you part with your parents?" Who knows how many other questions they asked us! They already knew our background, they were testing us. I remember having to explain to them that we were just like orphans because our parents could not take care of us and were both sick. This is how we entered in the world of children without family and they gave us a button that said: U.S. CHILD.

We were in the Naples camp for about a month while papers were being processed. My aunt Irene was in another part of the camp with the Canadian offices getting her papers processed for Canada. For some reason, she could not come to the States. She did not want to interfere with our placement and felt this was the best way. She also was very busy during this time and we did not see her. The fact we did not come together was a great regret in her life. We needed a placement in family and she needed work to get settled as an individual.

From Naples, we traveled across Italy into the Alps and arrived in Bremen a couple of days later. Of this trip I have very little recollection, perhaps because of the shock of leaving our parents and the trauma of this separation.

The train stopped in Bolzano and effort was made that our cousin, Nini, a young man now, who lived in this city, be there to see us for a moment while the train stopped. We only saw a glimpse of him as he was trying to come to the train on his bike. We only saw him enough to wave good-bye.

I can see now how children can be traumatized with a separation from their parents and then retain this fear later in life. At different times in life I found it very difficult to part with any one significant and even animals and objects, which have been part of my life.

We were in Bremen a short period of time, a few weeks. Here we were in a large army camp, probably used by the Germans during the war, now converted to refugee camp.

I remember walking to a large plaza in the camp where a lot of the refugees gathered. My sister and I and one Italian girl stayed together pretty much, probably for moral support. There were no other Italians. We were surrounded by numerous languages. No one spoke Italian.

Finally we boarded a small Navy ship called *James Stewart*. I recall, it could very well have been a similar name, but this is what I remember.

The ship was small and we had bunk beds three to four high. The mess hall was small and cramped, but I can still smell it, a special type of smell.

During the trip on the ocean, we had many days of very rough water and the ship would ride up on a big wave and then plunge down. It was scary. I was often seasick. Sometimes, to prevent the sickness, my sister and I would go on deck to the fresh air and sing at the top of our voice. Nobody could hear us with the roar of the sea. The singing seemed to help the waves of nausea and vomiting, most probably because we concentrated on something else other than our stomach. It kept our mind off the fear too.

During the meals, I would be very busy helping with the small children and also set tiny tables. My sister, being younger, was not required to work.

All the time I was in real doubt that we would ever land anywhere. I thought one of the times the ship would not come up again from the hole in the sea.

We finally arrived in New York. We marveled at the Statue of Liberty as we sailed into port. New York appeared like a magical city of lights. It was like a dream, we never had seen a city this big. We went through Ellis Island. Here was the usual wait and paperwork processing. We were all lined up going through offices. We were accompanied by adults who could speak for us.

We finally arrived at the youth center. I always felt so grateful to the people helping us, always smiling and talking to us in a soft voice. I felt welcomed.

I knew that real love and kindness was present in all the people that met us at the port and then took us to the center, which was in the Bronx. The people were happy with us. They wanted to make us feel liked.

On the trip from Naples, to Bremen and then to New York, I was only in a trance and performed all that was asked of me like a robot. Now in the center, I felt safe and responded to the love the people were showing us, and finally came alive again. I could see and observe people and think, while before I could not even think and was only walking, standing in line or just in trance.

Now I could feel inside me the warmth of people and the caring they showed. I could live now and maybe become normal. I was not afraid anymore.

I knew then as now that American people are so generous and so willing to help the unfortunate. A few years ago, there was an American couple traveling through southern Italy with their child. The boy was killed by bandits in an ambush. The parents, in their grief, decided to donate a part of the body, unheard of in Italy. I'm sure since that time Italians learned something different than they ever knew.

Happiness is working for the happiness of others.

One of our songs we sang on the ship:

Sta sera gli angeli non volano	Tonight the angels don't fly
ma piangono per noi	but cry for us
piangono perche te ne vai	they cry because you are leaving
sta sera gli alberi si abbracciano	tonight the trees hug each other
perche vogliono nascoderci dalla luna	because they want to hide us from the
amica del nostro amore	moon, friend of our love
Non dirmi che tomerai	Don't tell me that you will come back
perche non lo farai	because you will not do it
lo so che non ti vedro	I know that I will not see you
non ti vedro mai piu	I will never see you again
Fra poco tu te ne andrai	Soon you will leave
io so che piangero	I know I will weep
ma poi mi scordero di te	but then I will forget
Sta sera gli angeli non volano	Tonight the angels don't fly
ma piangono per noi	but weep for us
piangono per me e per te	They weep for me and for you

How appropriate for our fate, as we never saw our mother again, our dearest love. At times in our life here, we did forget, as it happens when young people are so busy with their life.

51

The Center

In New York City, the World Council of Churches either had the building as a gift or as loan from somebody rich. It must have been a grand old residence at one time.

It was three stories high and looked like a big house with so many rooms and a stairway to the front entrance. I vaguely remember the brief stay here, three months, and I only remember the first and second floor. The first floor was a large entrance adjacent to a big room. This was our main area, with many tables and chairs. There was a kitchen and dining room on this floor. I just can't remember any meals in particular, but everything was wonderful, even if different from any food I had at home in Italy. I remember Jell-O, something completely new to me. On the second floor were bedrooms.

What I remember most of all are all the children of so many ages, very small and toddlers, to teenagers. Since my sister and I were teenagers, we mostly associated with our own age group. Of about twenty to thirty children at that time, there were only about ten of our age, and only one other Italian girl about the same age. This girl, however, was going to some member of her family in New York City.

She was the only one who had some place to go. She had made the trip with us to Bremen and then to New York with the United States Navy ship we sailed on.

My biggest regret has been that we did not keep in touch with these children. We were all waiting day by day to hear where we would be going. We didn't even know any address until we got to our destination, and we were all going to different parts of the country. I didn't even know when anybody was leaving, but suddenly they were gone.

These refugee children were the ones we would have had so much in common with and we could have even been some support to each other in our new life. Life was flying by fast, I'm sure we all had a lot of adjusting to do with many problems.

Kicci (I didn't know how it was spelled) was a Hungarian boy of about fifteen. He had been at the center before us and he tried to be extra nice to us newcomers to the center. He would sit by us at the table, showing love by smiling and helping in every way. He was like a brother, almost as if he sensed our predicament. He was what we know as an old soul. He had compassion for us, our loss of our parents, and he tried to be a brother to us. He did not know our language, and we could not communicate in English, but his expressions were loving and showed willingness to help.

Kicci was a stocky fifteen-year-old, who must have worked hard in his short life. Even his hands were that of a worker, not a young boy. His Hungarian features, olive skin, dark eyes, his easy warm smile, reminded me of my mother. I told him that my mother was from Budapest and then he became especially close to us.

He accompanied us to the baseball games close by, where for the first time we were exposed to baseball. I didn't understand anything about it, but almost all the other children went as a group to the games and Kicci would always sit by us.

Another special boy was Gusty. He was Jewish and very small for his age of fourteen or fifteen. Still, his face was old. He seemed to be out of place somehow and I'm not sure what language he spoke. Words were not important at this point, I would understand so much more with their actions and expressions. There were certainly more boys than girls in the older group.

It seemed to me that almost every child spoke a different language, but sometimes, I could see two speaking to each other. The languages were Russian, Czech, German, Hungarian and even more but I could not tell what they were. Could have been Latvian and Finnish. We did not understand each other at all and nobody spoke English that we knew, especially not us.

We had been divided in different classes around the house, in different rooms, or different corners, to learn English. My sister and I must have been the worst in English, because Mr. Jim decided to give us extra tutoring. One important first sentence that we had to learn, according to Mr. Jim, was "I don't know."

One day when we were walking around the streets, someone asked us something. Of course we didn't understand anything, so we said "I don't know." the man looked at us very disgruntled while he kept on walking and pointing to his wrist. He had not pointed to his wrist before and we certainly were very quick with our new sentence. He wanted to know the time.

We had much free time when we would roam the city and take all the subways. We were always in groups and with the more experienced kids who had been at the center for a while and knew the city by then. We were somewhere in the Bronx and we became very good at finding all the other areas in New York City by subway.

Mr. Jim led us to his beautiful apartment to show us how to get there for our lessons. After that, we were experts in the intricate way to get there. Sometimes he would turn the television on. It was the first time in our life that we saw a television. He told us to listen carefully, and our eyes were glued on the screen. He often would ask: "Did you understand?" We didn't understand anything. Mr. Jim was the most outstanding character in my life then and even now I think of him as an amazing person. He was definitely unusually gifted.

Mr. Jim was tall, blond curly hair, a very good-looking man perhaps in his fifties, although I could not judge any older age then. Now thinking back, he may have been in his sixties. He was very thin and distinguished looking with perfect features, blue eyes, proportioned features. He was always impeccably dressed with clothes in good taste. He moved with grace and agility, and appeared aristocratic.

The amazing part about Mr. Jim was that he could speak all the languages perfectly. I found out to my satisfaction that this was true. He spoke Italian perfectly and in fact I was convinced that he was born in Italy, somewhere in the northern part where there are many tall and blonde people. He was a teaser and he would even talk to us some Italian dialect that only a native could have spoken. He led us to believe that he was Italian, always while smiling.

One day I managed to communicate with Kicci. "Did Mr. Jim speak Hungarian well?" This is a well-known difficult language to master. Kicci nodded smiling, "Yes, yes, he Hungarian." I knew that this could not be, he spoke Italian too perfectly. Then I questioned the Russians and the Latvians and the answer was the same.

On a day when Mr. Jim was giving us the English private lessons, I started to investigate with persistent questions. Finally, he said, "I am really English, from Britain, but I traveled all over the world." It was still hard to believe him because how is it possible anybody could speak so many languages without an accent and people could not detect any difference? I have never known another person like Mr. Jim in all my life. He was our link between all these languages. He spoke all the languages, including Russian and even Greek.

Our stay in New York City was short but memorable. One by one, all the children were being placed in different homes. It was sad to see them go and just disappear.

Our little group of two Italians, two to three Czechs, two Russians, a Hungarian, a Latvian—perhaps about six or seven of us, stayed close. I could not remember many of the names, because they were strange to me at the time, being used to only Italian names. I really believe there might have been a deliberate effort for us not to bond too closely however, as our lives would go in all different directions and as we saw parting was very sad. This was 1950.

When we become older, there is a stronger desire to have close friends. So many times during later years, I longed to see and talk to the kids of the center.

I missed Mr. Jim so much, and yet I did not attempt or know how to get in touch with him when he was still at the center. We loved Mr. Jim and we understood that he was very special. He was generous with himself, and he was a giver. I believe he was working for a good cause, where he spent all his days with refugee children rather than at a prestigious job. He had the talent of the languages and I believe he gave this gift in a very unselfish way. I don't believe he was working for money.

When I volunteered at the Olympic Games in the northwest (Tacoma and Seattle) in the eighties, I saw a difference. I was translator for the Italian Penthatalon. Some athletes asked me how much I was earning doing this job. They were totally surprised of my answer, unheard of in Italy for the majority of people, I suspect. They said, "No one in Italy would do this for no pay!"

We came to a rich and powerful country and we were proud to be part of it, but most of all we came to a generous nation, willing to help the unfortunate. America is indeed rich in spirit and willing to help and welcome the Displaced children of WWII, and encourage them to also make a good life.

It was a privilege to go to Mr. Jim's apartment for lessons. His home was spacious, overlooking Central Park. Many times we walked there with him, in his attempt to educate us in the American life, where families and all kinds of people walked. He would take his two white Afghan dogs. As far as I knew, he lived alone with his dogs.

Walking in the park was always after we studied and practiced the language. When we were there, it was study time and we could only glimpse the view from his apartment and the short period of television to see if we understood.

Still, as much as we were well taken care of, my main dread was that of the unknown. Where was everybody going? It was hard to see children leave, but when the time came, they were excited and we were happy for them. They were going to a home where they would be accepted. My sister and I were some of the last to leave. They asked us if we would separate. We had promised our mother that we would stay together no matter what.

The other Italian girl moved on quickly because of the distant relations she had right there in the City. The rumor was that although she was only sixteen, a marriage had been arranged, but I doubted it. Our sponsor, the World Council of Churches, would have never allowed the arrangement.

The older boys were able to understand they were going to states like Iowa, Nebraska, probably with farm families. The children were all scattered in different states to families willing to take them.

This life too had to pass and almost forgotten, but the

memories come back easily and all the faces pass by and I remember the perfect aspect of each personality. Life rushes on like a river, and we are carried in the current.

52

Suddenly, No Family

My sister and I came to this country with no family, had a deep shock and were only barely able to realize the extent of this fact. We were able to conceal the feelings of isolation by being involved in an entirely different life than we had ever known. We were in the midst of strangers, totally alone, and totally dependent on the two kind elderly teachers who gave us a home.

We were refugee children of WWII.

We had a close, nurturing family in our early years, now we had no one but each other. We were different, with different customs and background. The two teachers, our guardians, June and Winifred, tried to understand as we in turn also tried to understand them and our new life. The well-meaning teachers really underestimated our pride. At one point, they proposed an adoption, explaining that we would have to give up our name. It was such a shock, we would never give up our name for any reason at all. Even to this day, I can feel our reaction to the preposterous idea of giving up our family name.

Everybody we came across at school, church and everywhere, had some aunts, cousins, grandparents, etc., but not us. We were so busy with life, school, the language barrier that we could only partly take our minds away from our situation. We didn't know English because we had only three months of lessons at the New York City youth center. Language was offered in schools in Italy and I had taken French, the only choice in my grade.

It must have been inconceivable to the teenagers in school or church—two girls coming alone from another country. This was 1951. Not many foreigners at that time, at least not in Bremerton, Washington. As soon as we came to Bremerton in January 1951, we were enrolled in Bremerton High School, taking classes such as math, English, choir, typing, gym, Home Economics. We did not understand much of anything. We could understand math, typing, but following recipes and measures was a struggle. I had to ask for help from the teachers for every step of the way. As June and Winifred were devout Methodists, we immediately were introduced to the MYF, youth group of the church. It turned out to be a good experience where we made kind friends to last our life time. We were busy, but we still had no family. We came from nowhere as far as the world out there, school, shopping, or church. In those days, people did not travel much and Italy was a far away country. Some people in New York didn't even know where Washington State was, or at least they said that it was on the other side of the world, where people were still almost pioneers, a country full of Indians.

In 1950 we were in New York City for three months, waiting to be placed in a family. The World Council of Churches was trying to find a home for us, but in our parent's written agreement, it was stated that we were never to be separated. When we arrived in New York with the Navy ship, we were pinned right away with a button that said U.S. CHILD. I was fifteen years old and my sister was thirteen.

We had such a wonderful family and no one will know unless I write about it. We were not just two people coming here from nowhere, a faraway country. We were products of life and fate. Like a swift river, life runs to her destiny, the current will not stop, it will only go around the obstacles.

The intuition of my parents was correct. We found a new home and adjusted after many years. Their spirit is with us always, it gave us courage and strength. *"Life begins tomorrow."*

53

The Arrival

My sister and I were finally told that a placement had been found in Washington State. People and workers at the center were saying "poor kids." We understood they did not consider this to be a lucky placement. They felt sorry for us at the center.

Mr. Jim explained to us that it is a very faraway state, and with lots of snow and cold weather. Some people even believed this was still Indian country, with little wars.

There were very few little children left at the center. In our age group, all were gone.

We found ourselves on a train for at least three days and nights. I don't remember details of eating, sleeping, but I do remember the scenery. I was glued to the windows taking in all I could of this new land. It was all just so astonishing to me, even the large prairies as we went across flat lands. Then we came to the mountain country and the snow and I was amazed to see it so high near the train. I never seen anything like it, even in the little train in Pinerolo, where we had snow, but never so high.

When we finally came to Seattle, the train station looked exciting. I was anxiously looking from the windows to see the two ladies who were to meet us and take us to their home.

Stepping down, two nice ladies were very excitedly hugging us and also talking to us. Even now, with about three months of lessons, we could not understand anything and spoke even less, but we felt we had come to caring and warm people and to the end of our journey for now. The two sisters were even trying to talk to us in Italian, and had spent time learning enough to be able to communicate with us. The two ladies were June Nordquist and Winifred Dove, sisters.

From the train station in Seattle we started for Bremerton state ferries. This was another new experience, getting in a car and then in a ferry with car and all of us. June and Winifred were watching us all the time to see our surprise and reactions. We were just overwhelmed with so many new things. I found Winifred very serious and rigid while driving a big Nash, in comparison to people in Italy driving little cars with little effort, I used to watch cars whizzing by Riaglietto on their way to Sestriere to ski. Everything here was so orderly, getting into the ferry and driving so slowly and carefully.

In Bremerton, we arrived at a row of brick houses that lined the street. It was different from Italy, where housing was usually in large at least-two story buildings. It was different from Firenze, where the apartment buildings were really large, or Pinerolo in an isolated mountain villa, or back in Fiume with our house being part of two-story row building with many dwellings.

This Bremerton neighborhood had blocks of separated houses where seldom people were seen in the streets. People were just getting into their car in the garage on coming or leaving. This, of course, was wintertime when we arrived here. People are really isolated from their neighbor, or so I thought.

At the same time, we almost thought this was a little villa, with a very small garden and pond in the back. We felt very lucky.

54

New Beginnings

Life with June and Winifred was certainly different than our previous life. Now, there were schedules and rules. The sisters were teachers past middle age and taught in Bremerton High School. June was a widow and Winifred had been a Methodist deaconess who never married. Like so many other people, years later, I wished I understood their background better. As much as I could understand them, the two sisters were the children of a traveling man and their mother had died. They grew up with relatives in Montana and they practically did not know their father and knew very little of their mother.

The rules were all good, we were expected to eat at certain exact times, and all our activities were supervised. But I felt very much controlled and not free anymore. While in Italy with my family, I was very free to use my judgment and make decisions. There were no certain times to eat or go to bed. In other words, no one would tell us it was time to go to sleep or time to study and do homework. We knew what had to be done: eat what was available for dinner, then study or we would not pass our tests, go to bed so we could get up early to catch the little train to school in town. We had good upbringing when we were little and now we were entering teenage years and becoming responsible for our actions. In Pinerolo a lot of times after school, I had to cook some soup and some dinners. I knew what we had to do. Mother was coping with life as best as she could.

We now lived in a modest brick house, not far from the

high school. June and Winifred were very active in the Methodist Church, which was part of the World Council of Churches, I presumed. This is why they committed to the responsibility of taking in two teenage girls from a foreign country who were complete strangers to them. They felt safer to have some rules and routines by which to live now with us there. They had the same rules with their own children and in school as teachers. June had a grown son and a daughter. Winifred had a well-disciplined life as deaconess in earlier life.

Even in New York City, we were roaming the streets and subways all by ourselves. The people working in the child center were tolerant, trusting and knowledgeable of children's needs and behavior from so many different walks of life. Of course, New York City, in the fifties, was safer in those days.

In Italy, I was cooking just from observing my mother cook, certainly not from recipes, and only with ingredients available. Here, we were being taught cooking from a book with measurements I had never heard of. In Italy I improvised soups made from our vegetable garden. I helped my mother in every way I could as I saw her becoming more and more distraught. I knew she was thinking all the time that our life was not turning out well.

In our new home, we were told how to do everything, the simplest tasks. Winifred was especially strict with times to come for breakfast and time to leave the house for school, and expressed herself very firmly. I found it difficult to live so regimented. While before I was my own boss, now I could not be five minutes late for breakfast, and of course, I knew when to leave for school, did not have to be told again. I felt controlled when I was told in detail several times what to do. On the other hand, June and Winifred were very patient and forgiving with us. Once they scolded us very seriously because we went with some of the church group to see Elvis Presley on TV at somebody's house. We did not call to let them know what we were doing. This, after all, was a new way of life, reporting all our actions. They tried to make us understand some of these rules. We did not grow up with rules of this sort. At times, we were all hurt and Winifred especially talked to us and counseled us. We were always forgiven.

At Bremerton High School, June was in charge of the history and the social studies classes while Winifred taught mathematics and photography.

School was fine even if I felt like a fish out of water. There were stares as other kids were studying us, our every move, how we walked, and how we acted. They had never seen a person from another country.

Today, I know that even in Italy people do watch Americans, British or other visitors, and they even have a preconceived idea of each personality. They love Americans for their easy smiles, they have their own ideas of all the other foreigners. But then, I thought we were the only ones in that situation where we were under observation.

One time, during an assembly, a totally new concept for us, they had asked us to come to the stage and talk about our background: "What do I think of the clothes here?" and many other questions. I could hardly understand and answer, but managed somehow.

I said: "The saddle shoes look like boys' shoes and not very attractive." Everybody laughed. I don't know what all else was asked, but the whole time there was a lot of laughter after every answer, which was in very poor English, I'm sure. None of it was very funny to me and I hated to be in the limelight.

Our classes were the ones that we could possibly handle: typing, French (which I had taken in Italy), math and choir, also home economics and gym.

Mr. Manzo was a typical Italian-looking choir director, but he was not especially helpful or warm to us, keeping a distance that I interpreted as "Swim or drown." His primary vocation was to direct a choir of voices, with style and much facial expression. He had a special relationship with sopranos or the pupils that had a good voice he could always depend on.

We were tutored by June and Winifred at home, who were armed with an Italian dictionary. They had traveled in Europe and also wanted to learn Italian. It was not a bad idea: we needed to learn English and they Italian. But they sacrificed their wish so that we could learn English. They wanted us to learn English as fast as possible, so Italian became a secondary language. June and Winifred firmly said we now would have to talk to each other only in English. So we did and it seemed so strange and yet funny. We got used to it and to this day, we don't talk to each other in Italian.

There was one bright thing in the two years of high school experience. The other kids were mostly nice to us. One boy even accompanied us to school. Ron would also wait after classes to walk with us, His home was nearby. Charlotte would wait for us in the morning outside the door to walk with us to school. June and Winifred had to leave earlier in the morning for their classes. We joined the MYF (Methodist Youth Fellowship) group and made lasting friendships. To this day we have some close friends from High School days, like Marge and Tom and several others.

One American institution that was completely new to us was the concept of the allowance. We did not understand it at first, but eventually it was explained to us that we were supposed to buy new clothes for school with it. Instead all our allowance money went straight to Italy for my mother. While my father was taken care of in the hospital, she had no income. These were hard times for our parents and they needed the money a lot more than I needed new clothes. While we were immersed in a new life, our parents only lived for our not too frequent letters and the money was an assurance that we were doing well. I didn't see anything wrong in wearing the same clothes for several days because I did not get dirty. The other students did wear different clothes almost every day, which was strange to me.

After graduation, everybody went in a different direction, but often we would still keep in touch with some of the friends we made in those years. They knew us when we didn't even speak English. Throughout the years, we've tried to take at least one hiking trip in the summer, as we did in High School climbing club. In this group, Winnie was a warm and loving friend to us.

These first years of our separation were very hard for our parents. They waited for our letters. I'm sure they spent most of their time talking about us and waiting for our letters. Their sadness was made bearable by our writings saying we were doing fine.

While we were busy with a new life, our parents suffered. I could feel it from their writing and sometimes I'm sure there were dried tears in those letters they sent.

My mother's heart gave out in 1957 in Italy after seven years of suffering for us. Her only two remaining children gone from her arms, never to see again. My father died of a heart attack in 1967 almost at the same time of year, ten years later, here in this country. He also was sad in his last years, with our life evolving and he was often saying: "Your mother should have been here instead of me." He felt my mother should have had the joy of holding her grandchildren and being with us. He wanted to be of more help. He had a huge vegetable garden, and gave of himself generously to us. I wished I had taken his suggestion one time when he said: "You could work, if you like and I will take care of the children." But I wanted to be with them also, even at a cost of not having money of my own. Just a few years later, I wished so much for my father to be taking care of them when I worked. He was no longer with us. Another lesson in life learned too late. He had been able to emigrate shortly after my mother died, but that is another story.

*His grave has the inscription: "To give of himself is to truly give."

55

La Forza del Destino
(The Force of Destiny)

Mother often had said, "I will never be a burden to you." She implied that she never wanted to be a weight, either sick or depending on us. She wanted us to be free. I believe that is why she decided on the surgery. She knew the end result.

Our letters from America were not frequent and life was busy here. Mother understood. She knew we were free, we had opened up our wings and fled from her nest. There was no further purpose, her heart was not well, her legs were not well, and she had a low abdominal pain a few years. I heard it said that it was appendicitis, but not acute.

My sister and I were getting closer to having our parents join us here. We had been in the country seven years and had jobs and contact with people to help us with their immigration. I had lived with only this thought in my mind—to reunite with our parents. Their sacrifice and unselfishness was now to be paid with our family uniting here.

Without telling us in one of their letters, Mother went into the hospital to finally have the abdominal surgery before coming here. She would do this as she did not want us to be preoccupied with her because her wish was for us to take care of our life. Not to worry about her. My dear mother, she had risked her life during the war, always the constant nurturer, unselfish, she believed in her children to her last breath, and then she still worried to be a weight on us here.

One day, June and Winifred approached us hesitantly asking us to sit down as they wanted to talk. They had received a letter from my father asking them to break some bad news to us gently. Before they said a word I cried, "Mamma!" My mother had died! Suddenly, I had lost my most precious being, my mother, and lost a great part of myself. The emptiness I felt, the desolation and the loneliness, is indescribable.

Later, my father wrote some details of what happened. Mother had decided to go ahead with surgery on her abdomen, assuring father that it needed to be done before their coming here. At the hospital, in Torino all went well—a simple appendectomy without complications.

One evening after dinner, Mother was in recovery ward singing popular songs to the whole room. It was reported she sang so lovingly that everyone was moved with tears. They all knew her story, her dream of reuniting with her daughters. Two days after surgery, in the evening when my father was already gone home, suddenly while singing she put her hand to her throat and could not breathe. She died instantly of a blood clot to her heart. Blood thinners were not used in 1957 as they are today. Mother was sixty one. Life was just a dream, vanished in one instant. Like she said many times to me, "*e destino.*" It was predestined, there is nothing to do, the plan is already there.

My father later was able to reunite with us here and shared ten years of his life with us. His optimism carried me through and gave me the gift of "there is an other day."

Wind Beneath My Wings

It might have appeared to go unnoticed
but I have it all here in my heart
I want you to know I know the truth
I would be nothing without you.
                —A dedication to my parents and
                   my other mother, Bea Darlington

56
Representative Pelley

Five years after our arrival in the United States of America, my sister and I became citizens. We had learned sufficient English to graduate from high school and take the tests at INS. We had studied American History, which was completely new to us. Before we had studied only European History, ancient and recent, but never any American History. We were sworn in a ceremony at the immigration office in Seattle in 1956.

At this point, we began to give serious thought about arranging for our parents' emigration. When we broached the subject to June and Winifred, they were taken aback and surprised at our determination. They had just asked us to be adopted by them and change our name. We found this suggestion very shocking, because we had our parents, we were proud of our name. We appreciated the help the two schoolteachers had given us and we tried to repay them by doing housework and yard chores, but no one could replace our parents.

Caught off guard and incredulous of our intentions, they went to their wise and knowledgeable friend, Romaine Nicholson. She advised them to help us in our quest by contacting R.J. Pelley, who represented the Bremerton area at that time. Romaine was an interesting professor who seemed to know everything, especially about politics. Letters were written to Rep. Pelley, who was very kind and he helped with paperwork. I never met him and I believe only letters were exchanged with June and Winifred. He explained the steps we needed to take: to secure a job for my father and to procure sponsorship. A sponsor, as explained to us, meant someone to guarantee their stay here. I was already working at Zellerback Paper Company and was independent with a small apartment in Seattle. I thought this was sufficient warranty that I would take care of them. I never thought they would live anywhere else except with me.

Next step was to have a job lined up for my father. I decided to go to an Italian company and I went to Mission Macaroni, located in south Seattle. I saw this company on my way to work located in the same area. I just walked in the office requesting to see the person in charge. I presented my problem to the head of this company as best as I could. I remember this kindly man listening to me attentively with a soft smile. On the strength of my words, he signed the papers with assurance of a job in his company. I had now a work permit for my father.

Now I went to June and Winifred for the sponsor paper to sign. They hesitated and were even suspicious and did not sign right away. Eventually, they agreed to sign the paper after my insistence that I would always be responsible for my parents.

The health status of my father was cleared after his stay at the sanitarium. All these steps were certainly not easy, even with the help of Rep. Pelley, but he was a great help in speeding up the process. Even so, it had taken almost a year.

It was too late for my mother. She died in 1957 just a few months before all the process was completed. I never saw again her deep sad eyes, worn out by so many tears. I never would feel her kiss on my forehead. But her courage would be with me forever and so I had to work even harder now to save my father, who remained alone and lost. He came that same year by ship to New York.

This was a time when my sister Wilma also started working after she finished two years in Olympic College. We were living in a small apartment in Queen Anne when Father came over. Then Wilma, through some people at her workplace, was able to find another home for us. The owner of a small building on Rainer Ave in Seattle gave us a fairly large apartment with free rent and utilities in exchange for my father as manager. There were five or six apartments on top of small businesses and a bank. His job was to manage the boiler room in the basement, which supplied for the whole building. He was so happy, he finally could be of help to us.

Our life together started and it was like always, working for the good of our little family. Father was totally dedicated to us, even making meals for us, making our life so much easier.

57

Alone

My father had spent his days at the hospital in Torino where Mother was having abdominal surgery. The trip there was on a train for over one or two hours depending on the connections, from Abbadia Alpina, Pinerolo and Torino. Just one way. He would come back late at night, all alone in the dark to the old villa.

Two or three days after surgery, Mother sang her songs for the evening, her humble gift to the sick patients, before preparing for sleep. Suddenly some of the other patients saw her sitting up in bed, her hand on her throat, having trouble breathing. Then with a small cry, she fell back in the bed.

A small embolus became loose and lodged in her heart, and she was gone.

My father was devastated when he finally got the news. There were no telephones anywhere near our home and it was morning before someone was able to walk up the hill with the news. He had no family left and not many people that knew him in this new home. They told him to bring some clothes for burial. I remember my mother had prepared a very nice black dress, folded in a trunk and had told me: "This will be ready when I die." She really thought to take even this burden from us.

In a few days, one brother-in-law from near Venezia came to help.

There was the furniture and all household things they thought they had their whole life to dispose of. Father tried to save some significant items for us. He brought with him later in a steamer trunk.

Our mahogany furniture and the beloved Singer machine had to be given away. His life now was unknown and only the hope to reunite with us was what sustained him.

He could not live alone in the sad old villa, so far away from everything and the city. The two men worked silently together with all there was to do, including the funeral. After all this was done, he went to live with this brother-in-law and my aunt Elena, my mother's sister, near Venezia.

His own family, two sisters and a niece and nephew, were in Yugoslavia, unable to come for support. His brother in New Zealand.

On the outskirts of Venezia, in the town of Mestre, he tried his best not to be of any trouble to the small family, Aunt Elena, her husband and Franco, their only child. Elena's health was not good and this may have contributed to her not being hospitable and kind. Father would spend entire days roaming the streets of Venezia. This did not suit her and she accused him of spending time in *osteria* (pub). My father never had more than a glass or two of wine with meals his whole life. The very small pension he had was shared with them.

Finally, a distant relation and good friend of Mother throughout the years came to his rescue. They invited him to come to Palermo to their home.

These people, not even close relatives, were kind to him and convinced him that was the best place to await for papers for his departure to the United States of America to be with us.

I was working at Zellerback Paper Company and lining up all that was needed to have Papa emigrate. Finally, it all happened and we were reunited. I went to New York to meet the ship and it was easy to spot Papa because he had a big bouquet of gladiolis in his arm for us, a symbol of youth.

Papa's eyes were twinkling and he was so happy, but he could not help saying: "I wish I could have brought your mother." But despair was behind him now and he was going to start a new life with us. He always wanted to live for the moment and avoided dwelling in the past. He always adjusted to everything and always found a way to fix or turn into a better solution. I will always hear his words: "Be happy, nothing else is important."